# THE URBAN-INDUSTRIAL FRONTIER

David Popenoe, who edited this volume, also contributed a preface and an essay, "The Church and the Urban Condition." Dr. Popenoe is Director of Academic Affairs at the Urban Studies Center and Associate Professor of Sociology and Urban Planning at Rutgers University. He has also taught at New York University and the University of Pennsylvania and has written widely in the areas of urban sociology, urban studies, and social planning, and he has been a practicing urban planner in Philadelphia and Newark, New Jersey. His current academic interests are in community theory and social and cultural integration.

Edited by **DAVID POPENOE**

# THE URBAN-INDUSTRIAL FRONTIER

*Essays on Social Trends and Institutional Goals in Modern Communities*

**RUTGERS UNIVERSITY PRESS**
*New Brunswick    New Jersey*

Library of Congress Catalogue Number: 73-75680
SBN: 8135-0597-6

Manufactured in the United States of America by
Quinn & Boden Company, Inc., Rahway, N.J.

# Preface

David Popenoe

This book is aimed at urban social planners—and to a much larger audience which consists of everyone who is concerned about the direction toward which the social institutions in our modern communities both *are* and *should be* headed. It is made up primarily of a number of independently written essays * focusing on the major institutions in our society that impinge directly upon the daily lives of the individual and his family in the urban-industrial community of today and tomorrow. These institutions are the school, the church, the community government, cultural and social welfare institutions, and the institutional area of work and employment. They are viewed from the perspective of their changing functions in the context of the massive social trends of advanced urban-industrial society, and more especially with an eye toward the establishment of institutional goals—the most desirable directions on the urban-industrial frontier in which these institutions should be headed.

These essays do not propose immediate and detailed cures to the current "urban crisis." They are concerned with the more general and longer-run aspects of urban problems—with the basic

* Most of these essays were first presented in a lecture series sponsored by the Urban Studies Center of Rutgers University, the State University of New Jersey, during the 1966–67 academic year. That year marked the two hundredth anniversary of the founding of Rutgers, and the series—entitled "The Urban Frontier: 1966–86"—was one of the Urban Studies Center's contributions to the University's birthday celebration. The remainder of the essays were presented previously, mostly at the Urban Studies Center's annual Urban Issues Seminar during the years 1963–66.

ways in which our urban institutions must be changed if such
crises are not to linger long into the future. They deal in addition
with problems which are not yet dominant in the field of public
recognition, some of the emerging urban-industrial problems of
tomorrow. Thus they take a much broader view of urban problems
than most of the books, monographs, pamphlets, and articles on
this topic which abound in the country today.

This "longer and higher" view is sometimes still rejected by
intelligent people on the ground that it doesn't get to the *point;*
it detracts from dealing with the pressing issues of the moment.
Why invent new problems when presently we have so many
unsolved ones, the argument runs. Yet who cannot agree that
our current problems might be less serious if past generations had
only stopped to look ahead?

Each of the essays in this volume focuses on the future—either
by suggesting new goals that man *should* pursue in the future, or
in spelling out the trends which indicate the directions toward
which man probably *will* head, or both. In spite of the fact that
the orientations toward "should" and toward "will" are analyti-
cally separate forms of knowledge in a philosophical sense, they
are very closely related and indeed the average person has difficulty in keeping them clearly distinguished. They are much more
difficult to distinguish than, for example, "ought-should" from
"is-does" modes of thought—the orientations which roughly serve
to separate ethics, religion, and social philosophy from the social
sciences. The question of what is in human affairs may be capable
of verification in large measure by empirical science. This is not
the case with *what ought to be,* the subject matter of the more
normative disciplines. It is also not the case, primarily because of
the factors of human creativity and free will, with *what will be.*

The social sciences have not even begun to discover the "iron
laws of human relations" that would be required for accurate
social prediction, and most scholars maintain that no such iron
laws ever will be discovered. Nevertheless, the discerning of social
trends and their projection into the future has become a major
enterprise of late—representing in many ways a "new scientific"
version of the "historicism" and "social evolutionism" so prominent
in nineteenth century thought. While the latter modes of thought
concentrated on historical prediction through attempting to discover the rhythms, patterns, laws, or trends that underlie the

evolution of history (the article in this volume by Pitirim Sorokin is a later variation of this style of thought), much of the present futuristic thinking takes a somewhat "harder" line—with a heavy reliance on quantitative techniques and technological data manipulation, and a concentration on trends and changes that are visible in our lifetime. It is by no means yet clear that the newer approaches to the future are much more scientific than the older ones, but at the very least they are helping greatly to renew scientific interest in the big questions of human social evolution.

While the concern with "what will be" is associated with the social sciences, the focus on "what ought to be" represents in part an outgrowth of utopian thought—but the two modes of thinking are becoming increasingly complementary. Though over a half century ago Edward Bellamy was able to predict quite accurately the major structural outlines of the advanced nations in his utopian novel *Looking Backward,* one of the most important new developments today for utopian and other forms of goal-oriented thought is the increased knowledge of social trends being developed in the social sciences. Indeed the genre of utopian thought, which has been seriously undervalued and underproductive for many decades, also has been re-emerging recently partly under the guise of looking at the future in terms of social trends, and partly under the heading of examining the future in terms of desirable social goals.

Most of the essayists in this volume strive to achieve an integrated blend of the normative and the empirical. They have realized that the study of goals without trends gives rise to unrealistic "utopian" expectations; and the study of trends without goals gives rise to dehumanized and mechanistic scientism. Thus the balanced view of the future which is manifested in many of the following essays manages to steer a path lying between both the deterministic pessimism and the unwarranted liberal optimism that have characterized much earlier thinking about the future.

The order and arrangement of these essays also bears some explanation. The opening essay by Mayor Arthur Naftalin lays out the major dimensions of the problems of the urban-industrial frontier from the point of view of the older cities in our society. Though such cities by no means encapsulate all of the important issues, they are clearly the focus of most of our national attention today, and they include those problems the nature of which is best known. Thus the opening essay is intended as a bridge from the relatively known world to the perhaps lesser known and certainly more specific and detailed worlds that are portrayed in the essays which follow.

The second major section of the book consists of discussions of trends and goals in the six major social institutional areas: work and employment, social welfare, education, culture and the arts, the church, and government and politics.

The concluding section deals with some of the larger contexts in which these institutions operate. First, to keep the book "grounded" and "honest," is an essay on the problem of *paying* for our nation's critical urban-industrial domestic needs—and the relation of this problem to the national economy in the years ahead. The remaining essays cover technology and its powerful effects on every institution in the modern period; social and cultural values, which are the basic ingredient of every society and its institutions; and finally, the ever more precarious relationship between man-society and the natural environment in which and with which it functions. Each of these "larger contexts" is felt to bear critically on the shape and focus of the community institutions.

One of the interesting things about the modern age is that we seem to be at a point in history when two ostensibly conflicting beliefs are held simultaneously by a larger number of intelligent persons: one, that the chances are great that there will not be a future, and two, that we now are beginning to have the capacity to plan the future much to our own liking. This apparent paradox can be explained of course by the fact that the same factors that make for possible world explosion or annihilation also make for possible world control for human purposes. We are referring to the scientific and social technologies that make possible the city, the modern corporation, the cure for polio, and the trip to the moon, as well as thermonuclear warfare and extensive environmental pollution. These are the problems as well as the promise of the modern world, and they are probably the primary "causal force" behind urban-industrial societies. The scientific and social technologies are not, however, as many of the essayists in this volume point out, necessarily the "cure" for these societies' problems. The cure may lie not so much in the use of material or even social technologies—existing and yet to be invented—as in the condition of the hearts and minds of modern man: How he feels and thinks about things. The nature of man's concern for his fellow man may be far more important than the nature of the technological apparatus he may be able to invent. The control and direction of his feelings may be much more important than the control of his material environment.

Do these essays, which were developed quite independently by each scholar, emerge with any kind of common theme that transcends their particular institution or orientation? A general underlying theme which might be extracted from at least half of the essays could be stated as follows:

> The modern citizen finds a limited sense of personal and communal identity and meaning around his immediate family, peers, and private interests (such as his occupation); similarly, he is "plugged in" fairly well to his nation-state—indeed this is the only group in modern times, aside from his family, for which an individual is prepared to give his life (though this social fact seems presently to be on the decline). There is a profound lack of feelings of general identity and sense of community in *the middle range,* however, between the levels of family-occupation-corporation and nation-state. There are too few social ties and concerns bonding together the variety of social groups and individuals at the *local* and *regional* levels. A man's private and family concerns are too narrow and limited, his national concerns too abstract and depersonalized, to generate a strong commitment to the general welfare in the arena of the urban-industrial community.

This fact is basic in explaining the apathy toward the "invisible" poor, the weakness of state, regional, and local governments, the continuing permission of local environmental pollution, the insensitivity to community cultural and artistic expression, the ingrown and parochial nature of many contemporary church congregations, and many other themes that are explored in these essays. It is a fact that therefore deserves some elaboration.

The great motivation that has long characterized this country, the personal-familial pursuit of material and social gain, continues unabated in the modern period; a more recent companion to this is "let the government do it"—in those areas where the individualistic "free-market" order breaks down. The basic importance of both individual striving and the growing concern for "national interest" by no means should be minimized. But selfish private interest becomes immoral, and abstract national interest becomes shallow and somewhat meaningless, when these interests are not tempered by deeply felt concern for one's neighbor as well as one's self, for the larger local community as well as the neighborhood, and for "civic pride" in the region around us as well as pride of nation.

The intellectual's critique of urban man, which suggests that he is self-seeking, altruistically underdeveloped, and overconcerned with his own privacy, should not be limited certainly to the anonymous big-city apartment dweller. It applies with equal cogency to the metropolitan upper-middle-class man in his exclusive suburb, going back and forth between his job and the technological dream world inside his home—the only communal concern being a purely protectionist one. The fact that this individual is emulated by most of the middle class indicates the pervasiveness of this syndrome. The metropolitan world becomes one in which people who can't help themselves coexist near (but out of sight of) people who can give them the help—but who won't, because it isn't the American way.

Quite clearly, if we are to believe many of the essayists in this volume together with many other commentators on the American scene, the age of American individualism must come to an end. Self-interest and the acquisitive society based on this motive proved their worth in the industrializing period of the West— where the main goal was material advancement. This is not the main goal today in the advanced countries of the world. The goal of the urban-industrial frontier is *full* human development and not just material gain. It is moral, religious, artistic, psychological, and scientific advancement—in which further material gain may play in fact a diminishing role.

The search for full human development is not an individualistic but a communal enterprise. It is a communal enterprise not only because of the necessity for strong government as a mechanism of social efficiency—just as the large corporation is an essential mechanism of private efficiency in the individualistic order—but more importantly in the sense of the necessity for altruistic-communal concern to replace egotistic-individual concern.

This necessary "communal" social arrangement would seem to hold the key, also, to many of the "existential" dilemmas of our time—the problems of meaning and purpose in life. These problems have arisen not only because of the complexities of modern life, which are ever more difficult to comprehend, but more essentially because of the growing awareness that material goals are insufficient, that individual freedom is not the only major human value, and that personal self-gain is an admirable motivation only within carefully circumscribed limits and within a socially rewarding context. Possibly the fault lies, as Pitirim Sorokin's essay develops, in the fundamentally faulty, or at least highly partial, value and reality assumptions under which modern man operates—favoring purely empirical, logical, and secular modes of thought almost to the exclusion of all other modes. Whatever the precise diagnosis and prognosis, it is getting more and more difficult to find people on the right or the left—and now more commonly in the middle—who don't regard "progress" and the "modern period" as a mixed blessing. And it is regarded in this way precisely because of the problems of meaning, purpose, and identity—the psychological and moral tone of the urban-industrial order.

One might speculate that just as the Peace Corps solved these problems—at least partially and temporarily—for a limited number of today's youth, so altruistic and idealistic efforts of common concern in our communities at home could do the same for a much larger group of citizens, including those adult leaders who hold the power to act. This is what Long is referring to in part by his "local communities of common purpose," what Kahn suggests by his "patterns of cooperation and mutual aid around shared and common interests," what Boulding means by his "intermediate identity," what lies behind Taylor's proposals for a new educational philosophy, and what is basic to Sorokin's integral society and culture. It may be also, not incidentally, what many current politicians are groping for when they speak of the grave need for a new sense of national mission and purpose.

A highly frightening but rapidly growing feeling is abroad in this land today that the nation is going through a period of profound transition—one which at worst consists of a cancer in the vital organs of the American way, and at best represents at least a major setback to the achievement of the American dream. Some suggest that we turn back, but that seems out of the question. We must go on, and the institutional and societal reforms suggested in this volume hopefully throw some light on the path which inevitably lies ahead.

# Contents

# I The City in Urban-Industrial Society

# 1 The Old City and the Urban-Industrial Frontier

**Arthur T. Naftalin**

The modern forces of urbanism and industrialism are fundamentally altering the nature of life in every urban center in the nation. These forces constitute a far-reaching revolution that involves all phases of our national life; the "local" problems we face arise out of conditions that are national in scope—unemployment, cyclical economic movements, the mobility of our people, the unevenness of wealth—to mention only a few.

We must also recognize that the problems of urbanism do not result simply from the concentration of population in large modern urban centers. The problems are much more complex. They relate basically to the changing nature of our technology and our industrial society. Thus in seeking to develop answers to the problems of urbanism there must be a larger and deeper understanding of the forces that shape the new and changing institutions of modern life.

The facts concerning urban growth and development are now well known, and only a few figures at this point will remind us of their scope and immensity. Today two thirds of our population live in 212 metropolitan areas. By 1980 the proportion will be three fourths. By then we will have a population of 260,000,000, of which 190,000,000 will live in the metropolitan area. In less than twenty years, one half of all Americans will be living in forty great urban complexes. In short, the process of greater urban concentration is only beginning; the great movement to the cities is yet to come.

We have, therefore, only begun to experience the problems of urbanism. However difficult and challenging these problems may be now, they are most certainly going to intensify. It is not simply a question of adjusting to a larger number of people; the concentration in urban centers brings deeply unsettling qualitative changes. For example, much of the new urban population will come from farms as automation and our ever more productive technology reduce the opportunities for employment on the farms. This group of new settlers in the cities includes large numbers without productive skills, at least the type of skills that are needed in the industrial and commercial urban center.

Another qualitative factor of immense concern for the future of our urban centers is the number of young people who will be entering the labor force. During the next decade 26,000,000 persons between the ages of sixteen and twenty-one will be seeking jobs, and of this number 7,500,000 will not have completed high school, and 2,500,000 will have had less than an eighth-grade education. At a time when our economy needs fewer and fewer persons who are unskilled or semiskilled, the prospect of this large increase of uneducated and untrained persons seeking entry into the labor market is indeed ominous.

Still another qualitative change is the growth in the number of older people. In 1960 there were 16,000,000 people over sixty-five years of age in the country; by 1970 there will be 20,000,000; and by 1980, 25,000,000. With this growth in the number of elderly, many of whom are no longer able to hold productive places in the economy, comes an increasing need for public assistance programs and adjustments in the pattern of community life to provide wholesome and creative opportunities for the elderly.

A final qualitative change is the movement of large numbers of nonwhites into the large urban centers. Here again, many of these new residents do not have the kind of skills that make them readily employable.

Thus persons displaced from the farms, untrained young people seeking entry into the labor market, the elderly who are past the years that are regarded as productive, and nonwhites who have been deprived of educational and training opportunities—these make up a significant portion of the new urban population, and this adds up to a profound change in the character of our cities.

As these changes occur the cities of our nation are attempting to make effective adjustments, but the struggle is not an easy one because it is complicated by other factors. For example, my city of Minneapolis during the 1950s lost population despite the fact that the larger metropolitan area enjoyed one of the largest percentage growths in the nation. But despite the population loss the number of people over sixty-five years of age increased by 16 percent. Thus my city, like so many others in the country, is increasingly occupied by older people, many of whom live on small annuities or fixed incomes, and many of whom must have continuing public assistance. What has happened in our city is happening all over the country. As the children grow up they move to the suburbs, leaving their parents to live out their later years in the neighborhood in which they had lived during their active and productive years. The central city's population grows older; it loses the younger people who not only are in their most productive years but who provide the natural leadership that every community must have in evolving adjustments in the face of deep-seated change. On top of this comes the further complication that the central city, being only one municipality among many, finds itself governmentally unable to develop programs designed to meet the new conditions.

What has caused this profound population shift and the sudden eruption of interrelated community problems? Let me briefly review some of the underlying factors.

First and most important is the changing character of our technology. Our economy and technology are based upon the specialization of labor. Our society rewards the specialist whether he be a skilled worker, a professional person, or a business manager. As the technology grows more complex the importance of the person with specialized skills and specialized training increases and there is greater and greater need for coordination of and communication among the specialists who are engaged in common enterprises. Proximity and face-to-face contacts become more and more important, and the urban center becomes the focal point for such relationships. Men move to the cities because in a highly technical, industrial society it is the city that has the jobs and the rewards for economic enterprise.

With this technological growth comes a second and closely related factor, the sharp decrease in the need for men and women of no particular specialized skill. Machines replace the unskilled and the semiskilled; they drive the surplus laborer and manager off the farm, as I have already noted. Those displaced either remain in or are driven to the city in search of either immediate employment or an educational opportunity that will retrain them for some specialized task.

In the meantime science unravels more mysteries of nature extending the life span of millions of people, the very people in many cases whose labor—even if they are in good health—is no longer needed by the economy, because the labor they performed during their productive years can now be done by machine. As we have noted, an unusually large proportion of the older people remain in the city, and adding to their numbers come the older people who retire from the farms and leave the rural sections seeking companionship in the cities or wishing to live nearer their children who have already left the farm in search of new economic opportunity.

And just as science has extended the life span it has also reduced the infant mortality rate which, combined with the explosive birth rate since World War II, has produced an unprecedented growth in population.

Then, finally, there is another factor which has world-wide implications. This is the widespread cultural diffusion we are experiencing, namely the incresing glamour of the city. It is in the city that one finds the excitement of modern life. It is in the city that life pulsates and vibrates; it is the city life that is attractive and increasingly beckons young and old alike. Through movies, TV and radio, through books and periodicals, people all over the world—and certainly all over this country—have come more and more to associate the excitement of life with large urban centers. That's why they come to the cities. They come to the city because this is where they expect to find the full and rich life. You will recognize that this expectation is related to our high level of prosperity and to the general affluence we are enjoying.

Technology, science, affluence, and the quest for excitement—these combine to produce the new exploding urban frontier, and the frontier is here to stay. However you may feel about the rush to the cities and however painful it may be to view the formless sprawl that characterizes so many metropolitan areas, you must face the plain fact that none of the factors producing urban growth is reversible. You might wish wistfully that we could turn back the clock, that we could go back to a simpler time, to a simpler economy, that we could go back to the one-family farm, that we could go back to a different kind of role for the family, that we could somehow reduce the effect of the automobile. We will do none of these. All of the inventions, all of the machines we now have will stay; what's more, new machines—even more complex, producing even greater interdependence, a more penetrating symbiosis in our society—are on the way. There is no political effort, whether democratic or otherwise, that will reverse the course that follows from our science and technology.

The factors that are producing the new urban frontier are not reversible, and for that reason we must face rationally and courageously the problems and the new needs that result. Let me quickly indicate the range of the problems we must deal with in this period of profound change.

The most obvious problems are those that relate to physical growth—traffic, congestion, the construction of adequate freeways (freeways, incidentally, that are already inadequate before they are completed), parking, and mass transportation.

The population concentration produces problems of air and water pollution, and of maintaining adequate water supply and protecting that supply with effective waste disposal systems.

Space for recreational purposes is a need that we have only begun to recognize. In fact, the entire matter of effective land utilization becomes of imperative concern—new homes, new buildings, new freeways, new shopping centers, new factories demanding space, not just land to be used in helter-skelter fashion, but as a part of a rational and systematic plan.

Perhaps our most serious problem is the lack of sufficient educational facilities. As we have seen, education, training, and retraining must be provided on a massive scale if the people of our country are to acquire the knowledge and skills that our economy must have to progress and expand.

Inadequate housing remains a staggering problem despite all the building that we have completed since World War II. We are still far behind in this area.

Add to these the need for further airport development, more runway space for the ever-faster jets, and more terminal capacity for the growing volume of air travelers. And airports generate the problem of noise, an especially baffling problem that at this point concerns virtually every major urban center in the nation.

And, finally, as regards the problems of physical adjustment is the whole broad area of zoning, of proper land use, and proper controls—to be achieved by a democratic government in the context of a democratic society seeking to protect individual rights at the same time that the general community interest is being advanced.

But our physical problems are only a beginning. The social problems of the new urban frontier are even more compelling, more urgent. A new pattern of life is settling over urban America. For many communities the transition is loaded with tension, with the need to shape new patterns in human relations. Slum clearance, low-rent housing, freeways, and urban renewal bring with them dislocations of families and disruptions of neighborhood patterns. Migration, mobility, and the weakening of the fabric of family life are related to increasing juvenile delinquency and the rise in the general crime rate. Social dislocations and social disorganization intensify personal difficulties, and as a result the maintenance of mental health becomes a problem of community-wide concern.

In those communities having the most advanced form of social disorganization we find drifting gangs of unemployed young people, jobless and out of school, what James Conant has called "social dynamite." These problems of social upheaval call urgently for massive attention; they will not respond to superficial expedients.

The physical and social problems confronting our cities are worries enough, but beyond these concerns are the further complexities of an inadequate fiscal and governmental structure. As we have noted, our cities are growing older, large numbers of productive residents have moved to the suburbs, new freeways slash through the old central cities removing substantial properties from the tax rolls, and while the property-tax base diminishes the demand for services increases. Because of the cities' dependence on the property tax the increasing tax burden falls more and more on the older people who have remained in the city. At a time when the old city must reach out to meet the challenge of the new frontier, it finds itself hobbled by a tax structure that is inadequate and inequitable.

Thus, to complete our roster of problems we must add the problem of financing and the problem of our inadequate structure of local government. Solutions to all these vexing problems must be sought amid the bewildering structure of a fractionated and fragmented multiplicity of governmental units. Intermunicipal rivalries and competition for industry are the dominant note in the relationships among municipalities at a time when cooperation and coordination are most urgently needed.

What can be done to make our local governments equal to the challenges of the new urban frontier? There are no magical solutions. The remedies have been repeatedly prescribed, and I can only restate some of the more basic steps that we must take if we are to forestall breakdown and chaos in our urban centers.

We must first face the absolute necessity of large-scale planning, the introduction of control mechanisms that ensure at least a modicum of rationality in land use. There must be more—not less—active intervention on the part of government in relating the needs of a burgeoning technology to an exploding population and limited land area. I do not mean governmental intervention in the production and distribution of services and goods. I mean a more active and effective management of the functions that are inescapably and inevitably *public* in nature—traffic control, construction of highways, sewage disposal, public health, public safety, zoning control, and education.

We must move ahead, unfortunately, at a time when the larger public is not fully prepared to accept a larger role for government. One of the dominant characteristics of American life has been our essentially antigovernment attitude and outlook. Throughout our history as a nation we have sought to minimize the role of government. We have emphasized localism in politics, home rule, the long ballot, restricted taxing authority, and diffusion of responsibility among boards and commissions, and we have favored the creation of a multiplicity of governmental units. We have enjoyed the delusion that government is not really necessary, that what functions it does perform are of secondary value and benefit to those provided by the private sector of the community.

Now we are faced with the necessity of seeing government as the creative and central force in our community life, of recognizing that the demands of the new frontier will not be fulfilled by an unregulated and untrammeled private initiative. We must see now that genuine governance is essential to our survival. Americans have tended to place greater emphasis upon keeping government responsive to the preferences, interests, and whims of the public rather than upon enabling it to lead, direct, and govern. Thus there must occur a basic shift in attitude toward government that endows it with the capability of performing the fundamental function of planning and directing.

This changeover in public attitude toward government will not be easy to accomplish. It not only runs counter to deeply ingrained views concerning the role of government; it faces the further obstacle of the absence of a dominant power elite that might have facilitated such a shift. The factors that have brought about deep-seated changes in urban life have also had the effect of destroying the power elite that in every community once dominated its politics and set the tone and pace for change. As Professor Robert Dahl makes so clear in his study of New Haven, now the political power has been fractionated and diffused, here and there in some cities there will be found a dominant interest group still powerful enough to direct the community's governmental life. But, more typically, power is now shared over a widely diffused base, among labor unions, business organizations, professional societies, and citizens' groups of many types, and all manner of economic, professional, religious, and social groupings, each having a nibble of power but none with the big bite. This means, in short, that if the political process itself is not an effective organizer of the governing power the power doesn't get organized, and there is as a consequence drift and aimlessness; the energies of the community become unfocused, and a power vacuum develops at precisely the moment that purposeful community action is required.

We should note here that it is in good measure the existence of this vacuum at the local level that results in the ever-growing pressure for state and federal action. The state governments have not—and I fear cannot—respond to the demand; they have revealed themselves as almost totally helpless in dealing with the mushrooming problem of urbanism—not only helpless, but for the most part indifferent. In some measure the helplessness and indifference of the states has been due to our faulty apportionment that underrepresents the cities, but this is by no means the full explanation. The states' helplessness is related in larger measure to their competitive position with each other and to the inadequacy of their tax base. During the six years I served in a central administrative role with my state government I can recall our preoccupation with state responsibilities and our only secondary concern with assisting the municipalities. Like all state administrations we found difficulty enough in financing direct state functions without adding to our concerns the problems of the cities.

With the states in default and with local governments increasingly unable to cope with their problems without assistance the federal government has inevitably moved to fill this vacuum. If one examines the National Municipal Policy as adopted by the American Municipal Association, one finds an almost endless listing of urban needs for which federal assistance of one type or another is urgently sought.

While federal support will unquestionably continue to be of primary importance as our cities grapple with their problems, there are other steps that can and should be taken.

We must reform and revitalize the structures of government at the local level to enable them to become effective instruments of leadership and governance.

We must move aggressively to integrate the myriad units of government that serve one area; we must reverse the trend toward fragmentation of governmental authority in the metropolitan areas.

It is crucial, too, that the strength of voluntary organizations be fully mobilized in the service of the community. In my work as mayor I have been greatly impressed with the strength and vitality of these voluntary organizations. Often they are concerned only with limited programs of immediate and particularistic interest, but many of them are seeking to find ways of improving neighborhoods, of developing better educational programs, or solving traffic and redevelopment problems, or accomplishing other objectives of community-wide importance. These groups offer one avenue of great promise because they enable individuals to identify with projects and programs that reach beyond their immediate personal concerns. We should recognize the constructive service that many well-established organizations will perform for the community if they are encouraged to assume leadership and to educate their memberships.

We need also to attract into government and to involve in

governmental programs persons of large outlook and strong commitment. I think we are making progress on this score.

In recent years we have seen an increased number of people of ability, of skill, and of large outlook seeking public office. But we need such people in even larger numbers.

We need, further, a courageous reexamination of our structures and processes within government. For example, there is urgent need to reexamine the civil service structure; it has become a strait jacket, hobbling government in its efforts to attract and hold people of unusual ability. We need also a much more fundamental approach to the financing of local government. But there will be no solution to this problem so long as local government remains fragmented.

To make the needed progress there must be substantial support from state governments. Their assistance is indispensable in helping the urban centers to meet the new challenges. It is encouraging to see moves like the recent one in New Jersey where Governor Hughes created a state department of community affairs. An agency of this type can provide indispensable help in many areas by assisting local government in planning, zoning, housing, water supply, recruiting and training of personnel. It can assist local governments in mobilizing and coordinating their resources and in achieving coordinated action on city-wide problems. We need, in short, throughout all of our government massive attention to the problems of structure and process. Our governments must become competent to govern, to resolve conflicts, to make decisions, and to get action.

The need is especially acute at the state level. States must begin to assume their proper responsibilities. This is not easy to achieve because states feel so competitive with each other and because for so long they have avoided the obligation of assisting municipalities.

Finally, it is inevitable that so long as state governments are in default the municipalities will turn to Washington, and at the federal level the need for improved structure and better procedures cannot be denied. As a concluding observation I should like to deal briefly with the importance of education in meeting the problems of the urban-industrial frontier. If my experience as mayor has given me any firm and lasting impression it is the indispensable need to mobilize the intellectual resources in our communities. The greatest shortage our society faces is the shortage of brain power. We live in the midst of a gigantic paradox. On the one hand we face the ominous prospect of an army of permanently unemployable people—people who lack training or a vocation. On the other hand our economy desperately needs an increasing number of persons with professional and vocational training.

Our survival demands a massive increase in educational opportunities, especially at the higher education level. We need an increasing number of leaders and managers, highly developed and deeply trained persons who can fill the complex roles that are being developed by our complex economy and technology.

We need a new emphasis on higher education in all areas. If we are to meet the challenge of the new urban frontier we must do more than reshape our old cities; we must broaden and deepen the knowledge and insights of the people who make up our communities. We must educate ourselves for life in the increasingly more complex urban environment, an environment that makes us more and more interdependent, and that challenges our ingenuity and our resourcefulness at all levels.

I believe we are equal to this challenge. We should remind ourselves that we do possess in this great country enormous resources, that we have a technology that can reshape the entire material and physical world, and, above all, that we have a democratic ideology capable of lighting the way to a world that will genuinely serve the fundamental values and needs of mankind. The key to our future is our will and determination to meet rationally the new conditions of urban life so that our old cities can gather new strength for the challenge of the urban-industrial frontier.

# II Institutional Goals and Trends in Urban-Industrial Communities

# 2 Urban-Industrial Complexity and the Problem of Functionlessness

**Lewis A. Coser**

Some forty years ago the great English social historian R. H. Tawney set forth a number of ideas in his *The Acquisitive Society* that are still worth pondering. They will serve me as a convenient point of departure for what I wish to discuss here.

In his introduction, Tawney stressed that the time at which he was writing was truly a time out-of-joint and that in such periods the tried and tested designs for living, on which a community ordinarily relies, are no longer of use. In such times, he suggested, the community "must make a decision; for it makes a decision even if it refuses to decide. If it is to make a decision that will wear, it must travel beyond the philosophy momentarily in favor with proprietors of its newspapers. Unless it is to move with the energetic facility of a squirrel in a revolving cage, it must have a clear apprehension both of the deficiency of what is, and of the character of what ought to be." [1] The crisis we confront today has, to be sure, a character quite different from that England confronted after the first World War, yet Tawney's general approach to it, though not his particular treatment, might still be of considerable value to us.

Tawney's thought at the time centered upon the notion of social function. He used this notion in ways related to, yet slightly different—because more evaluative—from, the way it is now used in much of contemporary social science. He meant by function "an activity which embodies and expresses the idea of social purpose. The essence of it is that the agent does not perform it merely for personal gain or to gratify himself, but recognizes

that he is responsible for its discharge to some higher authority."
And Tawney then continued: "The purpose of industry is obvious.
It is to supply man with things which are necessary, useful, or
beautiful and thus to bring life to body or spirit. In so far as it is
governed by this end, it is among the most important of human
activities. In so far as it is diverted from it, it may be harmless,
amusing, or even exhilarating to those who carry it on; but it
possesses no more social significance than the orderly business
of ants and bees, the strutting of peacocks, or the struggles of
carnivorous animals over carrion." [2] Tawney's polemical thrust
was directed here, as in the rest of the book from which I have
quoted, against what he called the sickness of an acquisitive
society. He contended that in a highly competitive society
individual strivings for preferment, advancement, gain, and
success subverted the social purposes, distorted the sense of
human values, and undermined human community.

Though such acquisitive strivings and the attendant under-
mining of communal value is, of course, still very much with us,
there is another problem that had not yet come into view for
men of Tawney's generation but that is central for our age: there
are today millions of people who may very well want to make
a constructive contribution to the society in which they live, but
who are prevented from doing so because of the very social
arrangements in which they find themselves. In other words, the
problem I am concerned with in this essay is not, as in Tawney's
case, the fact that men are diverted from performing constructive
and useful purposes because of socially induced forms of acquisi-
tiveness, egotism, and greed, but rather that men who may be
initially endowed with at least an average sense of social responsibility are yet unable to make a social contribution because of
the position in which they are variously placed in society, and
because of societal arrangements so irrational and inhuman that
they block the pathways toward satisfying and valuable social
services.

I am referring to the growing number of people who have
been rendered functionless in our present state of society: the
aged, the adolescent workers, the men with low industrial skills,
the discriminated against, and the growing number of other
categories of men whose skills are—or are likely to become in

the near future—productively obsolete or obsolescent. All these, I contend, have become in our present society "superfluous people," burdens rather than assets. These are men who are all around us and yet whom one would like not to see. These are vast categories of forgotten people, or at least people one would like to forget about. And this, I would submit is a most perturbing state of affairs. Most official spokesmen in particular seem to have given up any hope or even desire to make these people into valuable contributors to our society and seem rather to have come around to the view that, at best, these are men who somehow have to be taken care of, as one takes care of domestic animals who have outlived their period of productive usefulness.

Not that this state of affairs is without historical precedent. In seventeenth and eighteenth century England, when the revolution in agriculture which preceded the industrial revolution led to the displacement of tens of thousands of yeoman peasants from their ancestral villages through the so-called enclosure movement, social history records the aimless wanderings of uncounted superfluous and uprooted men who trudged all over the English countryside and flooded the cities and towns in search of work. Before the new industrial modes of production came into their own, when production was still in the main conducted by the settled artisanal and handicraft methods of the town workers, these men too were functionless, superfluous—a burden to everyone, including themselves. These unwanted workers began to be absorbed into the economy only toward the end of the eighteenth century when factory production finally began thirstily to require hands to man the new looms and operate the new steel furnaces.

While in the late eighteenth century the new machine technology finally helped to absorb these superfluous men, the stark and ironic fact today, two hundred years later, is precisely that the machines that were a boon then, at least in this respect, have in fact helped to create the new types of superfluous men of whom I wish to talk now.

Most people are familiar with at least some of the data on the impact of automation on American production within the last few years, and with the changes of enormous scope that this has caused in our economy. A few telling examples chosen at random might suffice to indicate this impact: [3]

(1) In the chemical industry, the number of production jobs has fallen 3 percent since 1956 while output has soared 27 percent.

(2) Steel capacity has increased 20 percent since 1955; the number of men needed to operate steel plants—even at full capacity—has dropped by 17,000.

(3) The U.S. Census Bureau used 50 statisticians in 1960 to do the tabulations that required 4,100 in 1950.

(4) Bell Telephone has handled a 50 percent increase in business during the past ten years with only a 10 percent increase in personnel.

(5) Not very long ago coal mines gave employment to over half a million men; today only 160,000 work in the coal industry.[4]

Examples such as these could be multiplied indefinitely.

There are those ever-optimistic souls who contend that these facts indicate only short-term movements on the labor market, temporary perturbations which will in time be adjusted, much as earlier undesirable consequences of new methods of production have in due time been corrected. After all, it is asserted, higher productivity, while it may temporarily lead to the displacement of some workers, will in the long run open new job opportunities for those displaced. This, I believe, is a fundamentally wrong view—a view that stems from the untenable assumption that there is nothing new in history, that what has occurred in the past is inevitably bound to reoccur in the future. And as to the long run—Lord Keynes gave the appropriate reply a while ago: "In the long run we are all dead."

The fact is that those who are displaced today do not readily find new jobs in other sectors of the economy. Instead of relying on generalities, let us look at a concrete case study. In a recent book by Professors Wilcock and Franke, entitled *Unwanted Workers*,[5] an effort was made to follow up the work histories of workers in five Midwestern plants who had been permanently laid off because of the closing of these plants for a variety of technological and economic reasons. The authors found that a very high proportion of these workers either found themselves unable to secure any other work or were forced to accept lower-paying and less rewarding jobs. A year after the shutdown, 65 percent of the displaced workers in East St. Louis, for example, were still unemployed. These long-term unemployed workers had, in the main, certain characteristics in common: they were predominantly older workers as well as Negroes. It would seem from these data that once a worker over forty-five loses his job, he finds it exceedingly hard to secure a new one. In each city studied, approximately twice the proportion of workers aged fifty-five and over were unemployed for the entire year following the shutdowns, as were workers under thirty-five. When interviewed many of these men felt indeed that they were from now on permanently assigned to the industrial scrap heap. One of them said: "It's little better than shooting me to throw me out of a job at fifty-five."

To be a Negro turned out to be as much a disability as being older. Negroes had been hired last. After the shutdown, even though they were younger and had somewhat higher educational attainments than the whites in the sample, their long-term unemployment rates were significantly higher. In certain cities, twice as many Negroes as whites were unemployed for the entire period after the layoff. Clearly, to be a Negro in industrial America is a disability. To be older is a misfortune. But to be an older Negro worker is indeed a calamity.

What this study shows, then, is that unemployment does by no means affect all categories in the labor force equally. While certain categories of skilled younger and white workers might have relatively little difficulty in securing new jobs after losing employment whether because of permanent plant closures, as in the above case, or because of the more insidious effects of automation, this is not so in as far as other categories are involved. Optimistic economists are wont to talk of the labor force as if it consisted of more or less similar units which can be readily exchanged, shifted about, and reassigned at will. But this is an absurd as well as an inhuman way of looking at the matter. People are not readily exchangeable. A miner losing his job because of the introduction of new coal-digging machinery in West Virginia does not turn up tomorrow as a happily "readjusted" diemaker in Detroit; he is rather likely to wait out his destiny in his mining town, waiting for the miraculous, hoping against hope that somewhere, somehow, there will again be mining work available.

We have witnessed in the last decade a revolution in skills. And, as the automated or semiautomated types of production will continue to grow, they will continue to displace workers who are not possessed of the skills needed to operate them. The possibility of obtaining employment in one of the new fields will depend to a very large extent on the level of skill and education of the job applicant. Hence there will be fewer and fewer job opportunities for those who heretofore performed more or less repetitive tasks which can now be done more easily and economically by machines. We now hear a great deal about the promise of reeducation and retraining; even the federal government has belatedly begun to wake up to this. But what has been done so far is piteously insufficient and has not even made a dent in the problem.

As it is, this nation, at the height of an economic boom and aided by war production for Vietnam, has an unemployment rate of 4 percent. Moreover, a high proportion of these unemployed are not seasonally unemployed, or persons between jobs, but rather men and women who are more or less permanently out of jobs, more or less permanently condemned to be discarded. Whereas in 1949 only 6 percent of the total unemployment was long-term unemployment, the proportion rose to 11 percent in 1954, to 12 percent in 1958, and to 19 percent in May 1961. In May 1961, almost one in every five of the unemployed had been out of work for more than six months. In the same month, two of every five had been jobless at least fifteen weeks.[6]

What all this amounts to is the perturbing fact that America has developed a kind of dual economy. There is amazing affluence and prosperity in one sector, but this is bought at the price of suffering, want, and social injury in another. It would hardly seem necessary to dwell here at length on the material deprivations that long-term unemployment visits on those afflicted by it. Michael Harrington's fine *The Other America* has amply documented the fact that today some forty million Americans live in poverty, unable to provide for themselves and for their families even the minimum standards of living which we have come to believe characteristic of American life styles. The physical needs of these people are real and urgent, and one should not condone the tendency among certain social workers to "psychologize" everything and to talk of dependency needs, inadequate role performance, noncoping personalities, and the like while ignoring the urgent and compelling economic and material pressures that lie at the bottom of so much of all of this. In this connection one cannot but agree with George Orwell when he bitterly commented upon pious complaints about the materialism of the working class: "How right the working classes are in their 'materialism'. How right they are to realize that the belly comes before the soul, not in the scale of values but in point of time."

Nevertheless it would be a mistake to consider here only the material deprivations that are involved. As Harry Bredemeier and Jackson Toby have argued,[7] for an individual to be rejected because of his lack of skill, his age, sex, race, or physique does not only harm him materially—it stigmatizes him and attacks the very basis of his self-esteem. "The cumulative impact of many refusals from employers creates feelings of worthlessness and inadequacy," and hence undermines the sense of personal identity. This is especially so in a culture such as ours which has so much emphasized the importance of work in defining and evaluating a man. We still, in many a relevant sense, continue to accept a Puritan ethos that stresses the eminent importance of work as a measure of man's worth. We still share the Puritans' conviction that idleness is not just an economic condition but rather an evidence of sinfulness. Hence to be out of work is considered, by many of those who are unemployed, evidence of inadequacy and personal failure.

Everett Hughes, the foremost contemporary student of the sociology of work, has been instrumental in calling attention to the importance of a person's work for his experience of self: "A man's work," he says, "is one of the more important parts of his social identity, of his self; indeed of the fate in the one life he has to live, for there is something almost as irrevocable about the choice of occupation as there is about the choice of a mate."[8] So much is this the case, Hughes suggests, that when you ask people what they do, they are likely to answer in terms of "who they are," that is, they attempt to establish and validate their own identity by referring to the identity of their work in a publicly recognized occupational or professional category. This helps us to understand that the loss of employment involves much more than material deprivations, it involves the loss of social identity and the loss of a sense of function. The enormous number of people who have in recent years been displaced from their accustomed work, and who have been unable to find other stable employment, are not only considered "unwanted" by the world at large; they tend themselves to develop a sense of inadequacy, of uselessness, and hence to sink into conditions of permanent retreat or despair, withdrawing their affects from the social scene, limiting their vision to the immediacy of the here and now, gradually losing the capacity for planning and foresight. They tend to be buffeted hither and thither by the winds of circumstance, losing the capacity of valuing either others or themselves.

I have so far centered this discussion on people having lost their jobs through automation, but it would be shortsighted indeed to see them as the only unwanted workers in contemporary society. The fact is that there are now growing numbers of young people who, far from losing jobs, have never had any stable employment in the first place. In recent years, unemployment rates among adolescents have been especially high. A major proportion of these are, of course, young men and women who have dropped out of high school. The unemployment rate for such dropouts is now a staggering 30 percent. In earlier periods these adolescents would normally join the untrained work force that performed the unskilled labor then so abundant in the industrial economy. But the fact is that now the demand for unskilled labor steadily declines as industry becomes ever more automated. Unskilled laborers constituted about 15 percent of the total labor force in 1910, but only roughly 7 percent today. In other words, a large proportion of those seeking entry into the labor force without possessing special skills are bound never to attain anything but part-time and marginal or seasonal types of employment. James B. Conant found, for example, that in one of our largest cities, in an almost exclusively Negro slum, 70 percent of the boys and girls between sixteen and twenty-one were out of school and unemployed.

My focusing on a *Negro* slum in this last example was not fortuitous. The fact is that we note in regard to the young, just as with the older workers discussed earlier, that being a Negro adds very considerably to the normal hazards facing adolescents ready to enter the job market. Among Negroes, not only dropouts, but many high school graduates as well join the ranks of the unemployed. Conant found in another Negro slum, in the same age group, that while 63 percent of the high school dropouts were unemployed, 48 percent of the high school graduates were also unemployed.[9] Here again, it turns out that to be young and unskilled is a serious disability, to be a young Negro even with certain skills entails grave drawbacks on the job market, but to be a young unskilled Negro is, almost invariably, a calamity.

This is not the place for extended discussions of the dropout problem. But let me just say this: There is real pathos in our American school policy. Our schools are woefully lacking in many respects, they are very often, especially in lower-class areas, more concerned with keeping youngsters off the street and away from mischief than in a serious effort at teaching them. Nevertheless, they strive earnestly and desperately to prepare the kids to take some part in a democratic society. But these young people know only too often that this society doesn't need them. Many of these youngsters, sensing perhaps that even the relatively skilled jobs which they might be able to get if they graduate from high school will yet not be jobs that might give them a sense of fulfillment and accomplishment, drop out altogether. Thereby, as in a self-fulfilling prophecy, they make it almost sure that henceforth they will not be able to get jobs that will provide them even with minimal satisfactions. On all of this, Paul Goodman's *Growing Up Absurd*[10] is still the most important tract for our times. He helps us to adapt a new angle of vision on the problems of adolescents in our society and to understand that when they are negativistic, bored, disaffected, sullen, and unresponsive, this is not so much because of a failing in them, but rather a failing in us. We, their elders, have failed to provide them with satisfying work; often we have failed to provide them with any work at all—and it is hence hardly surprising that many of these functionless youngsters feel indeed that they are growing up absurd.

Now let me say a few things about another minority group that is at a severe disadvantage in contemporary America: the aged. First of all we need to realize that there are now many more of them than there were in the past, and that their numbers will rapidly increase in the future. In 1920, only one out of every twenty Americans was sixty-five years old or older; this ratio had increased to one in every eleven in 1960. In other words, whereas in the past the aged made up only a relatively insignificant part of a population composed in the main of the young and the middle-aged, increasing life expectancies have made persons beyond the usual retirement age a very significant part of the population. In the ten years from 1950 to 1960, the aged population increased by nearly 35 percent while the general population increased only 19 percent. The very existence of such large numbers of aged people no longer occupationally active, in a society so wholly committed to an ethos of work, poses a number of very serious problems.

There have been, of course, cultures and periods in which the aged have maintained positions of social eminence. In nonliterate cultures they have been the bearers of the accumulated wisdom and knowledge of the society and hence have had a high status. But even in many literate cultures the aged were seen as the transmitters and upholders of tradition and were treated with reverence and piety. This tends no longer to be so in modern industrial societies where the only tradition that is honored is the tradition of rapid social change, and where the older generation, far from being treated with reverence, is indeed treated with scorn. Cultures that stress change tend to institute a cult of the young—of those who embody the changes to come. These cultures neglect or even ridicule those who remind them of the past.

In addition, of course, cultures such as ours, which are so strongly oriented toward work and which, as we have seen, consider work the key area in which individual identity and worth is proved and affirmed, tend to treat as worthless those who no longer work.

Here we encounter a curious paradox; we tend to value work highly, yet we tend to exclude from participation in the work process many older people who mentally and physically might still be able to make major contributions. In other words, we tend to utilize a person only as long as he is able to perform at peak capacity in his work role—and so we waste entirely the various contributions men and women could still make, even after they have reached their peak capacities. Granted that a manual worker after, say, the age of fifty may not be able to do certain physical tasks as efficiently as he did them earlier, must this really mean that he is no longer able to contribute his share to the total work of the community? Is it really true that white-collar workers or professionals are entirely useless after retirement? The best proof that what we deal with here are largely social definitions of usefulness rather than true estimates of biological capacity is evidenced by the fact that in certain specialized callings we think it to be quite in keeping for a man to serve long after what is considered the habitual retirement age. Looking at the ages of Senators, top members of the Catholic hierarchy, and Supreme Court justices, one often has indeed the feeling that for them life truly only begins at sixty-five. . . .

It is often objected that, after all, older people do not really wish to work beyond their retirement age. And there are indeed studies among the retired in Florida or California that seem to indicate that these men and women are content with their lot and enjoy their leisure. Yet, without being able to document this in detail, I have the feeling that many of these satisfied responses only hide an underlying quiet desperation. To be sure, when no alternative modes of living seem possible, many of these people tend indeed to say that they like what, for want of anything better, they have to like. But I persist in believing that the growing number of aged in our society, increasingly forced into a ghettolike existence, cut off from living contact with younger people and given no way of making a contribution to society, may serve as another indication of the fact that we have created institutional arrangements that are highly wasteful as well as devoid of reason and humanity.

I shall conclude this brief essay with some more general comments on the problem of functionlessness in modern society. Commentators on the current world scene are often wont to rank various nations in terms of such indices as productivity, per capita production, industrial as against agricultural employment and the like. Such indices are useful indeed in many respects, but they also tempt us, by focusing too exclusively on quantities, to neglect concern for the quality of life in the various countries compared. They too often tend to gloss over the fact, moreover, that those nations which have indeed achieved very high levels of industrial development are still woefully short of having achieved comparable success in the enhancement of the quality of the life of all their citizens.

One might, of course, hold to a Platonic view of society and consider that what really counts is the material and spiritual well-being of the elites rather than of the total body of citizens. But such a view is abhorrent to men who hold to a democratic vision. For these men then, I would submit, the quality of the life lived by *all* citizens of the society must be a major concern. Democrats cannot accept a society in which the material, and perhaps even the spiritual, well-being of the majority is as yet achieved only at the price of material and spiritual deprivation of a significant minority. We cannot accept, I would submit, a Darwinian model of American society according to which the full development of those considered most fit to survive is bought at the price of the continued stunting of the potentialities of those millions who make up *The Other America.*

What is involved here, or so it would seem to me, is a basic reevaluation of our scales of values as well as of the use of our resources which is determined by such scales of value. If, indeed, our major societal aim is to beat the Russians in production statistics and in the race to the moon, then what we are presently doing is probably a rather rational way of allocating our resources. If, in contrast, our scale of values is informed by a truly democratic concern for all of our citizens, if, in other words, we take seriously the emphasis on equality and fraternity which is so important a part of the American creed, then, I would submit, we seriously need to reappraise and reorder our current scales of resource allocation. In this case crash programs for, say, the upgrading and reorganization of our whole educational system, especially for lower-class youngsters, would seem much more important than crash programs for beating the Russians to the moon.

Space does not permit me to spell out some of the major structural reforms that are needed in order to come to grips with the functionlessness of millions of our citizens. But I would like to warn that there is always the danger of so immersing ourselves in the concrete solution to this or that concrete problem that we may lose a sense of the magnitude of the whole. I think we must always keep before our minds the idea that what we have to deal with by far transcends the problems of this or that specific group of people. We are not in the situation of a doctor who has to deal with the particular problems of particular patients, we are

involved in a situation in which the whole society is in effect
the patient. The problems of functionlessness cannot, I am convinced, be attacked in any fundamental sense as long as we don't
realize that these are not just problems "out there," *their* problems, but that they implicate all of us, that they can be solved,
if at all, only if all of us cooperatively join in their solution.

It will not be enough to adopt toward them the traditional
social workers' approach, which is predicated on the idea that
we, the healthy, do something for them, the problems. We need
to realize that to come to grips with the issues that I have
sketched may require that we, the healthy, the affluent, the well-
to-do and well-adjusted, will have to make major sacrifices in
our own accustomed way of life in order to do away with the
scandal and the waste of human functionlessness. Paul Goodman
concludes his fine book by saying. "In order to have citizens, you
must first be sure you have produced men." If that be so, few
sacrifices that we may make would be more rewarding than those
that will help us to make men out of people who are now
drifting wreckage or discards.

All this, of course, is not meant to imply that detailed reform
is not necessary or important. In fact, if we focus exclusively on
large and perhaps Utopian plans we might easily be induced to
adopt a passive stance before immediate problems that may look
piddling compared to such large vistas. I have no doubt that
there are many detailed reforms that are likely to make some
contributions to the solving of some of the problems I have
sketched above, yet I am convinced that much more is required
here than such reforms. I do not believe, for example, that
occupational reeducation, even on a much larger scale than
currently available, will solve the problems automation now
poses for us. No matter how efficiently you are going to fit men
to the new machines and no matter how well you succeed in
upgrading their skills, you will still be left with the fact that the
total amount of work required in the society of the future will
be far less than that required in the past. For the first time in
human history, men will have to cope with the problems of what
to do with their vastly increased leisure. While all through
history, the majority of men have been preoccupied with work,
they will now have to worry about their leisure—about what to
do while not working. To cope with this, it would seem necessary

to throw over whatever there still remains of the Protestant work ethic. We will gradually have to come around to the view that monetary reward in an age of automated affluence need no longer be tied to productive effort in industry, as it needed to be in an age of scarcity. In such an age, perhaps, withdrawal from work areas need no longer entail the harsh sanctions of an earlier age. Why, then, not so redistribute our resources, as Robert Theobald argues in his recent *Free Men and Free Market*,[11] that those not inclined by temperament or disposition to engage in productive employments would still be enabled to live stimulating and rewarding lives? Perhaps those cultivating the arts of leisure may make more significant contributions to the culture of the future than those tied to the wheel of industrial production.

NOTES

1. R. H. Tawney, *The Acquisitive Society* (London: G. Bell and Sons, 1948), p. 2.
2. *Ibid.*, p. 9.
3. I have used a number of examples given by Donald N. Michael, *Cybernation, The Silent Conquest* (Santa Barbara: Center for the Study of Democratic Institutions, 1962).
4. Cf. Dan Wakefield, "In Hazard," *Commentary*, Vol. 36 (Sept. 1963), p. 3.
5. Richard C. Wilcock, and Walter H. Franke, *Unwanted Workers* (New York: The Free Press, 1963).
6. Wilcock and Franke, *op. cit.*, pp. 10–11.
7. Harry C. Bredemeir and Jackson Toby, *Social Problems in America* (New York: John Wiley & Sons, 1960), pp. 46–47.
8. Everett C. Hughes, *Men and Their Work* (New York: The Free Press, 1958), p. 43.
9. Quoted in Michael, *op. cit.*, p. 22.
10. Paul Goodman, *Growing Up Absurd* (New York: Vintage Books, 1962).
11. Robert Theobald, *Free Men and Free Market* (New York: Clarkson N. Potter, 1963).

# 3 The Frontiers of Education

**Harold Taylor**

Most of our public discourse in this period is about disasters and failures of various kinds, large and small scale, about the pollution of air and water, the corruption of public sentiment, failures in education, the rise of protest and violence, hostility between nations and people, the conflict of public bodies within the American society, the rigidity of Boards of Education, the attrition of credibility in the present Administration and, to put it most broadly, the erosion of the world's confidence in itself and in its ability to deal humanely and peaceably with humanity's problems.

But in all this public turmoil, a central element in the cause of our discontent is seldom mentioned. It is that one of the reasons for the turmoil is simply that we have a lot more instantaneous public information to have the turmoil about, that millions more of the world's people have joined in what was formerly a fairly private and slow-moving discussion among members of an elite who made their own decisions about how the world was run, that new expectations and new demands are now being created by whole new sectors of American and world society. To choose an example at random, that is what makes Negro parents boycott bad schools and riot in the slums.

Looked at from the perspective which I now recommend, we can consider the present unrest in the American community and everywhere in the world as the inevitable consequence of the breaking up of an old order and the transitional stage into a new order in which the poor, the ignorant, the uneducated, and the deprived are demanding that their rights be recognized and that societies be reorganized in such a way that these rights be fulfilled in reality. If they are not fulfilled by intelligent, compassionate, and cooperative social action, they will be achieved by force and violence.

This is what has been shown in Watts, in Harlem, in Bedford-Stuyvesant, in Chicago, in Cleveland, in San Francisco, in Calcutta, in Djakarta. We have not yet learned to achieve, as Adlai Stevenson said in his last public address, "impartial protection for the whole wide society of man."

This is what is at stake and this is what makes man's new agenda different from the old. We are now accustomed, for example, to talking about and thinking about the idea of poverty because the problem has thrust itself into our consciousness, because we are now conscious, here and abroad, of the disparity, in a total sense, of the condition of the poor in relation to all others. Poverty does not mean the absence of money. Poverty is a name for that condition of life that prevents a man from gaining the benefits of his own society and from fulfilling the possibilities that lie within him.

We can take pride, and a certain amount of cheer, from the fact that this country is now making a serious effort to remedy that condition by the use of national resources in money, manpower, and brains. That we have thereby stirred up a host of other problems as we apply ourselves to the task is unavoidable, but in a way necessary, since we are bound to learn a great many things about modern society and how to cope with it that we never knew before. That is now the frontier territory for American education.

I cite one sentence from an American public figure to lead to the problems which lie in that territory: "We in America today are nearer to the final triumph over poverty than ever before in the history of any land."

This is not Lyndon Johnson's sentence. It is Herbert Hoover's, speaking on August 11, 1928, not very long before the crash.

There is reason to believe that we *are* nearer to a triumph over at least some kinds of poverty than we ever were before, partly because we are at last tackling the problem, and partly because we now know that we have to tackle the problem through education.

That is what Hoover and the others did not see. They saw the affluence of the educated well-to-do and mistook it for a state into which all men might come by the genial drift of capitalist history and by the sheer initiative of a nation of free enterprisers. The men of the 1920s were blind to the fact that without an educational system that gave everyone a chance to develop his talents, including the talent for having initiative, neither the social nor the economic system would work. They both depend on the educational system.

It was Horace Mann who put that matter straight. "Education," he said, in his classic American statement, "beyond all other devices of human origin, is the great equalizer of the conditions of men—the balance-wheel of the social machinery . . . It does better than to disarm the poor of their hostility towards the rich; it prevents being poor."

This is exactly what the turmoil is about—to create an equalizer of the conditions of men. New York City has not created such an equalizer. Neither has Los Angeles, Chicago, San Francisco, or Cleveland. What has happened, as is usual in education, is that the social changes and the new demands they generate have far outrun the capacity of the educational system to keep up with them. The progressive philosophy holds that education should not only anticipate social change, but should help to bring it about by staying close to the growing edge of social need and close to the personal reality of each child, in the context of his family and his community.

For the progressive in the 1930s, this meant a philosophy of public education that conceived the school and its curriculum as centers of creative energy and moral concern in which children, their teachers, and their parents worked together to develop new ideas for the enhancement of life in the community and thus for the enhancement of life in America and the world at large. It was Whitman's *Democratic Vista,* Emerson's *Man Thinking,* Dewey's *School and Society,* put together in an ideal for learning that stirred the imagination and commanded the energies of a generation of scholars and teachers. The school was intended to be a community center where all kinds and conditions of humans could come together to learn from each other—Negroes, Italians, Irish, Germans, Catholics, Jews, atheists, Chinese, Protestants, slow learners, fast learners, artists, Midwesterners, Southerners, and even plain white native American New Yorkers.

The distance we have skidded down the slippery path to that ideal can be seen in the fact that we now talk so much about education for the disadvantaged, remedial reading, corrective arithmetic, integration techniques, compensatory education, speech clinics, tutorial centers, After School Study Centers, Evening Projects; so much talk of so many special remedies that I often wonder why in God's name we don't set to in full force and do the things *during* and *in* school so that we wouldn't spend such incredible amounts of money, time, and energy trying to undo, redo, and add to what obviously is such a miserable and unproductive way to spend a child's time in the first place. In place of the ideal of community, with the school at its center, we have created a situation in which parents have to fight, storm, and struggle, even to have themselves recognized as worthy of attention or capable of giving useful advice in the conduct of the affairs of the school in which their children spend their days. In place of the educator with a free style like Eliott Shapiro, of P.S. 119 in New York City, in whose school "teachers felt free to experiment and in which they could depend on [further] support from an actively interested parent body," we have put a premium on administrators who can keep things in order and get as many children as possible through the tests at grade level. In place of creating situations in which the child can find a way through to himself and his world, we have blamed the failure of his education on his environment and on the child when, in fact, the failure is in the schools.

A great deal of the trouble comes from two sources—the absence of a philosophy that can give a sense of direction to educational action, and the failure to recognize and to welcome the fact that a whole new sector of American society has begun to assert legitimate demands which have until now been ignored or frustrated.

Both these matters are connected. Education has come to be considered by the public and by educators in these last years to be an academic exercise carried on in schools and colleges where you go to get academic credits, pass tests, get grades and certificates, and to establish your credentials for a place in the society. Without the credentials you have no place.

This is a European, class philosophy, suited to producing and sustaining a class society, and is favored by, among others, Admiral Rickover and his followers. The educational system is to be used to screen out the academically unfit, retaining those who have had the privilege or good fortune of good preparation for secondary schools and colleges. The trouble with an elite philosophy of this kind is that it does not make very good arrangements for the ones you screen out, and after a while you have something happen, like the French Revolution.

The point of view, however, is now generally held by the University academic hierarchy who control the high school curriculum by controlling the entrance requirements to college, and is also generally held by the public who want their children to succeed. Teachers, in this conception, are therefore considered to be persons who, in the classroom, administer the courses, which have to do with books, tests, quizzes, and preparation for more academic studies in the next grade up. That is why the certification of teachers has become so dominant a part of their preparation. In judging teachers, ability in passing pencil and paper examinations and tests has been substituted for ability to enter the lives of children in a way that can help them totally.

Along with the idea of academic screening and incessant academic testing goes the idea that there must be an authority in charge of the students and the children in their curriculum of studies and in their lives in general, an authority that makes the rules and sees that they are carried out. This follows logically, since if education consists in learning academic subjects, they have to be administered as the handing on of the word. The school board therefore hires a superintendent to carry out policies it sets on behalf of the society. The superintendent hires and inherits officers to carry out board policies as he sees them. The principals, under certain constraints, hire teachers to carry out the policies, and the system that results is, quite simply, an authoritarian system.

Here is a frontier for new research in educational planning—operational research that can develop new kinds of schools in which the parents, the teachers, the children, and the principal work in cooperation to make a new context for the school in the community. The new movements in developing a new approach to teaching in the inner cities include the concept of community development in which the total context of the community is considered as the educational setting for the school. If the school can be considered as a community center, and if talented parents without formal education can be brought into the center as teacher-aides, educational organizers, and community leaders, this adds a strengh to educational programs without which it is impossible to function.

In a similar way, bringing in student-teachers from the colleges, and men and women who have themselves been educated formally but have not taught, providing them with an internship under supervision of skilled teachers, can give an intellectual and social content to what otherwise would be a humdrum system of the usual single classroom with one teacher and the usual curriculum of standardized subjects.

Linked directly with research and new planning to bring a community dimension into the life of the child, is the possibility of serious reforms in the education of teachers through making the experience of community life a part of their preparation to teach. The conventional pattern of the education of teachers is to isolate them in college classrooms where they study academic subjects for four years, with education treated as an academic subject, and a semester of direct experience with teaching reserved for the senior year. This quite often makes it impossible for a student who has been trained to be a teacher under this system to accommodate himself to the situation in the inner cities, which then have the problem of the recruitment of teachers who are both interested in and trained for the difficult work in slum schools.

The frontier of experiment in this sector lies in the programs of the National Teacher Corps and of VISTA, where the conception of teaching is considered to be that of rendering public service in a community rather than teaching subjects in a classroom. The National Teacher Corps curriculum calls for internship in a school under supervision of experienced teachers while university studies are carried on in fields directly related to the problems of the schools and their communities. In the case of VISTA training, the educational value lies in the immersion of the student in a culture with which he has usually been unfamiliar in the past, and where he finds direct information and knowledge given to him from members of the unemployed and uneducated groups with whom he is associated.

This is a style of education for teachers that needs to be extended beyond its present confinement to specialized training for teachers of disadvantaged children. Every teacher needs to have the experience of a culture other than his own, and no matter where he is eventually to teach. The experience of service in Head Start, VISTA, the Peace Corps, or inner city schools is one which gives him a quality of experience of crucial importance in his development as a person and as a teacher who understands the structure of his own society.

What I would propose for work in this frontier area is simply that teaching and education be considered to be a form of national and international service, as the responsibility of all citizens, young and old, and that the enormous energies and resources of the younger generation be brought to bear on problems that they are willing and able to solve. There are 250,000 high school and college students across the country who are at work as volunteers in tutoring children in the inner cities and rural slums. Many of these volunteers are learning to be teachers without formal instruction, but with the supreme advantage of learning what it means to serve others in the exact dimension of their need. Others of this generation are serving as teachers abroad, in the International Voluntary Service, and at home in dozens of projects of the students' own devising. As of now, little has been done to build parallel programs within the universities, programs through which students could learn what it means to teach by working daily with children.

Why do we not take the central idea of the Peace Corps, VISTA, the National Teacher Corps and the other volunteer movements as the basis for the radical reform of the education of all teachers? This is William James's *Moral Equivalent of War* joined to practical programs, in which the challenge of service in a high cause draws together the moral impulse of the young and the intellectual discipline of learning to cope with the reality of social problems.

To me, a liberal education is best achieved by the use of one's mind to understand and to act upon the problems of human existence. The sciences, the humanities, the arts are the means through which we can come to grips with the nature of our own lives and of the world in which we exist. What better way of coming to grips with that existence than by teaching whatever it is we know to those who know that little less than we do which makes all the difference?

This would argue for a new conception of formal education in school and college, a conception by which the student is not continually pressed to receive what he is given, but is continually asked to understand what he has learned by teaching it to others. Why not arrange on a systematic basis for high school students to teach each other, to tutor children in the elementary schools, as a regular part of their own curriculum? Why not ask our college students to work directly with high school and elementary school pupils, after school, evenings, weekends, during school hours, on whatever may be the problems that obstruct their intellectual and emotional growth, on whatever subjects in the curriculum in which they most need help?

I can recall vividly a young high school tutor in a volunteer program in Harlem who had dropped out of school and had been recruited as a volunteer in teaching Spanish. I asked him where he learned such fluent Spanish. He said, "In the streets." He was one of the most successful of the tutors recruited; he is now in college.

I have recently seen the results of a Peace Corps training program for Nigeria run by a young Peace Corps returnee who took ninety new volunteers into the Negro ghetto of Roxbury, Massachusetts, where the volunteers lived with Negro families, studied the problems of the Roxbury community, did practice teaching in the schools and learned to adapt themselves to a culture vastly different from their own by living and learning in the practical situation of that culture. This suggests the idea of resident student-teachers, store-front colleges, community-action projects of college and high school students together, foreign students joining with their American counterparts as teachers of foreign languages and history, sponsorship by colleges of education and by universities of study centers in the community itself where faculty supervision of new educational programs could make full use of all existing resources.

The impulse of reform-minded students in tackling these problems and other ones in the mass society is to act on their own, and to substitute for the conventional school and college curricula programs of their own invention. They are making a specific return to various forms of small group democracy, in an effort to work with indigenous leadership in whatever situations they find themselves. For example, the students at San Francisco State College have, over the past three years, formed their own Experimental College within the larger framework of their campus, to meet intellectual and educational needs which are unfulfilled in the larger system. The students have built their own internal college, not by fighting the college administration but by developing their own plans and carrying them out, teaching their own courses to each other and to the community, and in a sense educating the faculty and the administration of their college to understand their point of view.

Another group of students from the National Student Association have developed a plan for a poor people's college to be taught entirely by student volunteers recently graduated from college. The plan calls for rental of space in the middle of the ghetto in one of our major cities, a group of twenty-five student-tutors who would build a curriculum for the people of the community—adults as well as high school dropouts or graduates—based on what the tutors discover to be the educational needs of the people themselves. There would be no formal classes until individuals could be grouped together on the basis of their common interests and needs, and though it would not be the purpose of the students to prepare people for entrance to college, this might be one of the results in the case of those who are interested in going on with formal education.

Another variation of this idea is to be found in the experiment of the Womens Talent Corps for a College of Community Services in which the indigenous leadership in disadvantaged areas would be invited to attend a college organized in terms of the needs of the community, ranging from classes in reading and writing, history, problems of local government and democracy, with new curricula developed from materials of relevance to the intellectual and social growth of those in the program. The aim of the program would be to prepare people to take an active role in the community services.

The frontier area here is that of a developing program of education which expands beyond the formal school and college program and works outside the regular educational system. Yet it is

the most promising source of educational reform and fresh thinking we have about the educational needs of the United States,
since it deals with the actual needs of the society for specific
kinds of intellectual and social growth. It brings together the
two aims that must underly all serious education, the aim of increasing the intellectual possibilities of the individual being educated, and relating his education to a use to which it can be put
in the society at large. In the absence of creative thinking by
educators on the question of what to do with a population that is
ineducable by standard means, these new experiments outside
the educational system are producing effects that will have a role
in changing the schools and colleges themselves.

With the help of the mass media, a new generation now forms
a sector of society that is making new political and social demands which must be recognized. The young are no longer willing to accept the authority of the older generation or the authority of its educational system. Mario Savio, as political and educational leader in the Berkeley protest movement, is a symbol as
well as a factor in the response of the younger generation to contemporary culture. Stokeley Carmichael represents, within the
civil rights movement, a similar refusal to accept society and its
regulations in the terms in which they are presented to the young.
Five years ago, the ideas and opinions of such twenty-four-year-
old students and civil rights workers could not have achieved
national attention. The difference now is that no matter whether
the society agrees with them or not, young leaders like Savio and
Carmichael have formed their own constituency and speak to the
concerns of a subculture that in former years was invisible.

If we are to solve the problem of higher education and its use
for social betterment, we will have to take account of the criti-
cisms that the reform-minded students are now making of the
society and its educational system. Where these students have
been taken seriously and have been invited to bring their energies
to bear on educational and social problems, they have found
solutions unavailable to faculty members and administrators who
have been trying to go it alone.

I turn now to the largest frontier of all, the area of world
education. If the content of the curriculum in the schools and
universities of the world is analyzed, it will be seen to be the

product of national and regional conceptions of history, the social sciences and the humanities, designed to give each generation, in the part of the world it occupies, a sense of identity with its own traditions. This is of course a necessary part of any educational system. But at this stage in world history, the inherent nationalism of the separate curricula is dangerous to the development of understanding between nation-states and between ethnic and political groups.

Progress toward a deeper understanding of what is needed in the reform of American education to give it a world dimension has been remarkable over these past few years, since it has been achieved in spite of the tensions that now exist in world society. The signing of the International Education Act of 1966 by President Johnson marked a sharp break with past conceptions of the role of American education in the world order. The International Education Act calls for a shift in philosophy according to which American culture is considered to be part of the cultures of the world, and American resources are to be used for helping the citizens and their children to understand the problems and character of cultures other than their own.

At the present time, the best available statistics show that only 5 percent of this country's high school students have ever studied any culture outside the West, and that this is approximately the same percentage of teachers who have, in their preparation, carried on studies in non-Western cultures or history. In this connection, the most remarkable new development is that of the Peace Corps, which has proved to be an innovation, not only in diplomacy but in education. The Peace Corps is in fact a college for education in world affairs. Since more than 60 percent of all those in the Peace Corps are carrying out teaching duties in foreign countries, and nearly half of those who return from Peace Corps service are interested in entering the teaching profession, we have here a new possibility for the expansion of the Peace Corps idea directly in the middle of teacher education. As is the case with the National Teacher Corps, Head Start and VISTA programs, the central concept in the Peace Corps is the crossing of a cultural frontier. This has the double effect of helping the person who studies abroad or in a culture other than his own in this country, to understand himself by learning to compare his own traditions and values with those of another social and cultural group, and to broaden the range of his own knowledge in looking at the problems of the world and of his own society.

In New York State, the efforts of the State Department of Education in the field of world affairs have provided examples for the other states to follow. Through a systematic series of seminars in foreign cultures, the establishment of an International Studies and World Affairs Center as part of the state system of higher education, New York State education has taken the leadership in developing both plans and projects to add a world dimension to the education of New York State students. Plans are under way to make it possible for students in the universities of the state to study abroad in programs organized by one of seven regional centers around the world.

Antioch College, whose experiments in work-study programs have been an important part of the educational reform movement of the country, has approximately four hundred students each year studying abroad and has formed a pattern of alternate work on the Antioch campus in Yellow Springs, Ohio, and study and field work elsewhere in the country and in other parts of the world.

The concept here is crucial. The college campus is a staging ground for expeditions by students into the world at large. Students can then learn to understand the reality of social and cultural conditions and bring that reality to bear on the studies they carry out at home on the campuses. This approach to world education suggests a concentration on the problems of the world's cities. It is in the cities that the major cultural and political trends around the world are developing and where the problems of modern society are to be found at their most extreme. The cities are at the center of educational, political, and social change. This therefore argues for the establishment of world urban teaching centers here in the United States to which would come students, scholars and teachers from foreign countries to work with American counterparts on the problems of the inner cities. Following the pattern of the exchange Peace Corps by which foreign students come to work with Americans on community development projects, a world urban teaching center could test out new programs of education in the community of the kind suggested in this present chapter, and, by reason of the exchange of ideas and the practical work together between foreign students and

Americans, a direct flow of ideas about foreign cultures would be made available to the American schools and colleges.

In other words, the frontier of education lies at the edge of world society, beyond the boundaries of class, race, economic position, scholastic aptitude, or geographic regions. It lies in the problems of the world's cities where the major political decisions of the world are at this moment being made, and where the world's millions are congregated. If there are to be solutions to American educational problems they will have to be found in the cities, where the manpower—for social service, for technological invention, for scientific advance, for social planning, for political leadership—is to be found and where, as yet, that manpower has not been mobilized for a total reconstruction of the way things have been done in the past. In this reconstruction, the future of world society is at stake, not merely the correction of those social evils we have found among ourselves. If we use to the full our human resources, so bountifully provided in the energies and talents of the younger generation and in the untapped talents of the as yet uneducated, and if we support those resources by funds now available in an increasingly affluent society, we can join with the educators of the world in showing how to find remedies for the ills that plague us all.

# 4 Challenges to Social Work in Urban-Industrial Society

**Alfred J. Kahn**

Under a variety of banners, social practice, social science, and politics have embarked on a new social crusade. "Organize the attack on urban poverty," some state. "Create opportunities for upward social mobility," is the way others phrase it. "Rebuild the gray areas of our cities," urges a third group. Or, in still another vocabulary: "let us enhance people's opportunities to participate meaningfully in their society as a way of overcoming the tendency of urban-industrial society to make people 'functionless.'"

Whatever the specific concept or slogan, there is some degree of consensus about the general locus of a major social problem to be addressed: the mass of underprivileged, often minority group, members of the gray areas of our cities, concentrated in the unskilled segments of the labor force, living at the levels of poverty or deprivation, rearing children who are not equipped to grasp educational-vocational-social opportunities, and therefore holding little hope for the future. The resultant concentration of social deviance, pathology, and disability in these groups is taken for granted by the population at large. The high social cost is bemoaned but accepted as a necessary evil—occasionally to be attacked and then restored again, since alternatives are not acceptable.

Among those concerned with this continuing state of affairs, some see in this generally sketched social problem *the* issue of our age. Earlier social service commitments and preoccupations should, in their view, be thrust aside. It is, to them, not merely a matter of new *frontiers* but of new *definitions* of task and problem. Others, however, would attempt to retain what they consider to be sound, and to recognize and add new orientations and tasks in the light of what they see as new insights and new urgencies.

Confronting both of these groups, those who represent social work are called upon to suggest the degree and manner in which social work as a profession and social work as a social institution can be counted upon in these changing times. Precisely what is implied in the profession's alleged commitment to the humanization of the urban-industrial environment?[1] Is it reasonable to expect change and reform in a group which has not always been able to meet some of its moral commitments in the past?

A review of the history of social work as a profession and the social service agencies and institutions to which it has provided leadership discloses a fluctuation between two polarities. Social work has been involved both in (a) institutional reform and change and (b) the provision of supportive-rehabilitative therapeutic services within existing institutional structures. The predominant tendency in the twentieth century has been in the latter direction, of course, despite some feeling that this may not be entirely appropriate and despite some notable "action" exceptions and a small degree of dedication to building up areas variously called social change or social policy.

In fact, the general post-World War I social work preoccupation with remedial and therapeutic interventions lead to a view of the profession that relates it primarily to social welfare programs which come into play only when the normal primary institutions and the forces of the marketplace have broken down. This has been called the *residual* view of social welfare. Inevitably, social work was seen as a helping, liaison, therapeutic, rehabilitative activity. Its clients were perceived as casualties, failures, victims, or deviants in a world of generally self-sufficient and self-sustaining individuals. The assumption of this view is that social welfare programs and social work services are basically temporary and transitional.

In recent years, however, another perspective has been articulated which has become known as the *institutional* view of social welfare.[2] In this view, society should take account of technological and social changes which alter the relationships of man both to his primary institutions and to the general social environment. New social "inventions" should appear in response to the new functional prerequisites of life which arise in this changed social environment, and these new inventions are as "normal" in their way—in their relationship to the changed circumstances—as were the originally developed primary social institutions of a primitive agricultural economy. They are not, in addition, to be considered temporary or transitional. Social insurance, public housing, services to the aged, day care services, counseling programs, to give but a few examples, may be seen in this light as a social response to new challenge and circumstance. To stigmatize or penalize the user is no more rational than it would have been to call a nineteenth century American farmer excessively dependent because of the many ways in which he counted on the other members of his family and primary group.

Social work professionals generally identify themselves *intellectually* with such an institutional concept of social welfare, and its consequent implications for a broad definition of their profession. They are seldom challenged in this view except by staff of some sectarian programs or by lay attitudes among the untrained who hold social work jobs. The picture is often somewhat different, however, in regard to board, community fund, or lay volunteers who in some places stress the charity-philanthropy concept of social work and whose views of client-problem-program may best be described as residual.

In addition, the social worker's intellectual comprehension does not necessarily translate itself into a "balanced service model." Whether because (a) he works in a society in which the pervasive Puritan ethic supports a residual view, (b) his exposure to voluntary agency board or public officials often accentuates their residual concepts (and they ultimately control the program and budget) or (c) his training and skills have been oriented to clinical functions—the social worker is most often a *clinician.* Trained manpower and resources in the welfare field at the present time are heavily deployed in the direction of therapeutic, rehabilitative, or supportive services, and not in the direction of institutional change and social invention, despite impressive new forays into organizing, advocacy, and planning activities.

The institutional concept is translated by many professional social workers, therefore, into a commitment to guarantee social services as *right*, to make it possible to use help *without stigma*, and to assure that there are *enough services* to meet current needs. From this point of view—and to the distress of many of the "new crusaders"—it is an accomplishment to create family counseling programs and clinics, or homemaker programs and day care, which are acknowledged to be of use to all citizens and which therefore attract and hold members of the middle class, as well as serving more traditional client groups. From any point of view, of course, it is certainly progress to expand resources, to stress rights, and to define the use of social resources and services as normal in an urban society—and not as proving a user's inferiority.

When most social workers talk of prevention, as I have noted elsewhere,[3] they inevitably mean secondary prevention: early case finding and treatment before problems become serious. Like many people in the field of health, their model of social improvement-prevention is bounded by concepts of disease and pathology. They do want to block development of problem and disability but find it difficult to spell out in a positive sense what is meant by "enhancement of social functioning"—a social work equivalent of the doctor's "perfective medicine." I have proposed the concept of *developmental provision* (or *social utilities*) as a way of expressing this positive notion, a matter to which we shall return at a later point.

To summarize the argument thus far: The potential contribution of social work to the humanization of urban-industrial life and coping with the severe social handicaps of large segments of the urban population is somewhat ambiguous. On the intellectual level, an institutional concept of social welfare is now current which is a prerequisite to the making of an important contribution; but this concept has been most effective and completely realized to date in relation to *attitudes* toward *rehabilitative* services. In addition, prevention is still too narrowly conceived, in spite of this new institutional conception. While the institutional view would support both an improved *clinical program* (available as right and without stigma) and a program of *expanded developmental provision* (based on a measure of significant institutional change), it is the former that has been the primary thrust of social work in recent decades. As we shall see, however, there are now important prospects and expectations in regard to the latter—and these constitute the greatest challenge to social work in the coming era.

### SOCIAL WORK AND EXPANDED DEVELOPMENTAL PROVISION

If one defines the social work profession as ideally contributing both to social change and to the organization of special services for those in difficulty and in need, it is appropriate to look at what *is* and what *might be* in regard to each of these goals. Admittedly the present situation is unsatisfactory both in policy and program, and the difficulties lie in domains broader than those assigned principally to social work. Otherwise, there would be no cause for the present ferment.

Let us begin then, with the first of these two areas: social work in relation to social change. It will be noted that this paper has tended to employ two different conceptions of this "broader" role of social work. We have talked of a contribution both to general institutional change and to the creation of new social utilities (developmental provision). To some degree, this distinction may be one between ends and means, but it obviously goes beyond this. It is possible to support the developmental provision goal in a largely *status quo* context. On the other hand, it is also possible to see the need for new developmental provision in a context of social change characterized, for example, by equal opportunities for members of minority groups; increased citizen participation by those who have in the past had to leave most community decision-making to the more advantaged; considerably expanded social planning at the level of neighborhood, city, region, state; and the introduction of social dimensions into broader reaches of national public policy. While it would be difficult to generalize about the total social work profession with regard to all of these arenas, it is safe to say that most social workers are interested in something more than increased resource provisions in a *status quo* context. They know that adequate resource development and true access to new facilities are made possible only in a context of some social change. It would appear proper in this section, therefore (focusing on the urban social environment), to discuss illustratively several different forms of developmental provision which exist or might be sought as *goals,* as well as some activities or means designed to bring about the necessary change.

The thesis here is simple: Social change creates new prerequisites for adequate social life in urban-industrial communities. These necessary prerequisites ought to be socially created in the same spirit that earlier societies invented public roads, the post office system, public health, and public education because, like these earlier utilities, they have become functionally necessary to the larger society. The user is "citizen," not "client." There should be no personal defect implied in the need for the service, and no penalty involved in its use. These new social inventions, designed to meet the "normal" needs of people arising from their situations and roles in modern social life, can be thought of as "social utilities" or "developmental provision," as I have suggested above and elsewhere.[4]

This point might be clarified by talking of those *social utilities* necessary to today's city dweller which are comparable to the more traditional public utilities. We might mention programs such as the following, for example, variously sponsored by settlement houses and charity organization societies (now family service agencies) between the 1880s and World War I, and often continued to the present day: day nurseries or day care; penny banks; classes in English or various crafts; vocational guidance; family life education; camping. In the past, however, many of these programs were conceived as vehicles for the moral reform and reeducation of their users and they were directed at limited segments of the population.

Today's social conditions create new priorities. Much discussed are day care and homemaker programs which are good illustrations of new and high priority social utilities. The rationale for these is as follows: Many mothers work or are otherwise under circumstances in which they are unable to provide adequate all-day care to preschool youngsters; others wish access to a group experience for such youngsters as a socializing-educational experience. People with funds purchase such services. Many others lack access. Day care should be seen as a family strengthening and socializing *social utility.*

Similarly, actuarially predictable family emergencies such as illness, chronic handicap, or the limitations imposed by advanced age in an urban society in which many people are far removed from family or close relatives—or in which many women outlive their mates by many years—demand a variety of social inventions to support daily living. Homemakers and home helps (the distinction is not here relevant) can do much to aid a family in an emergency so that children need not go to shelters. Home helps can (often by devoting only a few hours per week to a person) keep an older person living in the community, and out of an institution.

There has been much interest in services such as these in the United States in recent years, but the development is quite limited in contrast to what has occurred in some other industrialized countries. Sweden, for example, with a population less than that of New York State, has more homemakers than all of the United States. Social workers here are now urging expansion, but the concept of what is needed too often leans toward the residual. The service is defined in therapeutic-rehabilitative terms, the user must be screened diagnostically, and the scale of service expansion remains limited. In 1962, Congress for the first time authorized federal aid to day care, but the concept as enunciated was clearly in the residual direction. One must be "diagnosed" as in need before one has access; this is no fully developed social utility. "Head Start" was also conceived in a residual sense.

Social workers continue to wrestle with this kind of issue, however, and more social workers are being won over to the broader concepts of day care and homemakers. Clearly, a firm commitment to the humanization of the urban environment demands that a high priority be given to programs such as these. Social workers should be ardent advocates of expansion. They may continue to have significant roles in the administration of such services, but it would be in error to urge expansion only in therapeutic-rehabilitative systems, i.e., day care or homemaker as social service, not utility.

A similar case could be made for a related service: the emergency baby sitter. Is it not time that the city dweller had access to a resource more routinely available and reliable than the teenage baby sitter or the neighbor exchange arrangement for a function whose requirements grow out of current living conditions? Is it necessary to spell out the consequences for personal health (parents need rest, change, diversion), involvement in children's education (parents need to attend PTA and adult classes), emotional security (children and parents need to be comfortable about the substitute arrangement for brief periods—shopping or clinic visits—or longer periods which may occur several times a week), deriving from the fact that some mothers never have secure arrangements for the care of their children, no matter how urgent may be the other demands upon them?

Another high priority social utility to be developed is an information service along the lines of the Citizens' Advice Bureaux (CAB) in England. This service has spread throughout England since the War and is now recognized there as a necessary part of community life. Variations of this in a number of other European countries and now in this country indicate a general recognition of the urgent need to undo or minimize the "ignorance factor" and to cope with bureaucratic rigidities in the urban environment. Here I should like to quote from an earlier book of mine: [5]

The Citizens' Advice Bureaux seem to have solved the problem of stigma which would face an "open door" agency associated in this country with a welfare program or a court structure. The key to the solution would seem to be the readiness to provide simple information about laws, procedures, and channels (even visitor's information in a tourist center like Westminster), while at the same time serving as a case evaluation center and referral unit in complex parent-child problems or instances of considerable personal disturbance.

A substantial portion of a bureau's time and energy is devoted to interpretation of legislation. . . .

. . . The experience of interpreting legislation to the public is paralleled by the responsibility to help interpret client problems and circumstances to government departments. In addition, when a government agency finds that correspondence will not suffice in dealing with a citizen about a complex matter, it may ask the bureau to help with explanation.

Inevitably, these roles give the bureaus a strategic vantage point for assessing the effects of new legislation, for making policy recommendations to local and national government, and for advising on the preparation of many types of leaflets and pamphlets to be issued by government departments.

Symptomatic of the importance of the CAB as a source of information in a welfare bureaucracy and as a channel for feedback to policy makers and administrators is the recent British government decision to increase substantially the rate of subsidation of this "voluntary" enterprise so as to permit more work in the field of consumer protection. While many issues remain (paid or volunteer staffing, intensity of work on personal problems, etc.), the CAB obviously have already demonstrated a constructive role.

American social work has done much with more narrowly conceived information services. The focus generally has been on social and medical services at the local community level—a reflection of the preoccupation of social welfare councils in the past with coordinating local health and welfare services. As one seeks to expand the service for the citizen at large, the focus should shift to housing, consumer problems, education, social security, and related areas. One would not want to decrease the expertise in the assistance-treatment realms, and we might expect that to the extent that these are seen in the perspective of the broader role, inquiry and referral will carry less stigma and case finding will be enhanced. (I have argued elsewhere about the potential of an advice center for unbiased case channeling which avoids getting a potential client into any specific service system before it is clear just which one will best serve him.)

Broader information services have been and are being organized in a variety of ways, but a pattern appropriate for the American metropolis has not yet emerged. Recent programs have tended to tie information of a limited kind to individualized service, a plan which may miss the advantages of the CAB pattern. This is an obvious field for new creative programming.

Since the intent here is to be illustrative rather than comprehensive, only brief mention will be made of several other types of developmental provision such as:

—new types of family (or adolescent) vacation resources
—new opportunities for peer experiences for adolescents, including group trips, cultural-educational activity, and camping
—new supports for induction of young people into marital life and help after birth of a first child (to include information and guidance in furnishing and maintaining an apartment, furniture loans or grants, practical nurse's aid after a child's birth, consumer information, and more adequate family planning information)

Beyond this, of course, one might enter into the whole income maintenance area and discuss predictable social statuses requiring financial support through insurance-grant-pension systems.

Many interesting alternatives currently are being discussed, but details cannot be elaborated here.

### NEW PRIMARY RELATIONSHIPS

Social workers, whether in casework, group work, or community organization, have always considered *skill in improving social relationships* as central to the profession. They also have a widespread awareness of the various forms of alienation which are now so common in the city. It is reasonable to expect, therefore, that beyond the therapeutic and rehabilitative tasks now accepted in social work practice, more emphasis will be placed by group work and casework practitioners, plus those in community organization, on that area of institutional innovation that focuses on primary relationships in the urban environment.

Indeed, there are already promising beginnings. In working with tenant organizations, antipoverty corporations, neighborhood self-help programs, model cities, and community mental health programs, public welfare community organization projects —or as detached workers with gangs—social workers are aware both of concrete programmatic objectives (achieving better schools and playgrounds, a new program facility, more adequate public services, etc.) and of the contributions of the change process itself to the achievement of stronger human relationships.

This is perhaps an optimistic perspective. Some social workers have placed the entire emphasis in community organization on the "process and relationship" goals and have underplayed concrete facilities and policies as targets. Others push only for resources and do not seem to display the much written-about skills in enabling. There is evidence, however, that the profession's main thrust will encompass both the process and the goal-oriented facets of planned change. Further, if one of the solutions for the modern city's tendency to render some people "functionless" and alienated is a new emphasis on primary relationships in urban neighborhood or housing development, then it seems important to build further on what some social workers already are doing well.

Though I do not mean to ignore here the research data which suggest that the nuclear family group in the city may not be as isolated as implied by earlier sociological literature, city man often does live in a world so impersonal as to deprive him of important attachments and guidelines. Whatever the details of continuing familial ties in the city, there is desperate need to create local neighborhood relationships and cooperative experiences which will personalize the environment. This may seem to be a romantic notion which would seek to undo the realities of urban life. It is, if the image is one of an all-inclusive neighborhood organization which has all of the functions of an extended family. What is realistic, however, is to seek those patterns of cooperation and mutual aid around shared and common interests that will assure both the achievement of important concrete objectives and the development of positive experiences in human relationships. Without these patterns, there will be a continuing expansion of the value desert which is at the heart of the problem of so many city dwellers. With them, existing community norms can achieve added potency and may come to reflect new social values. While the core of these efforts is and must be with the residents of disadvantaged neighborhoods, I see social work also contributing in this domain to middle-class neighborhoods and perhaps even to some unattached and socially lost young adults. In addition, work of this type is already underway that attempts to meet the special needs of senior citizens.

To be more specific, several new kinds of things seem immediately desirable, beyond present social work commitments to settlement, tenant council and local welfare council programs—and beyond social work staffing of those neighborhood self-help endeavors addressed to local needs and change efforts. (a) One of the promising possibilities for the neighborhood of the future is a pattern of old-young reciprocity. As senior citizens retire at younger ages, or have longer leisure periods in each work week, it will be increasingly realistic to expect young couples to turn to them for the guidance, baby sitting, and mature contacts which are not immediately available from their own parents, who are often not close by. Social workers could do much to encourage such a pattern. (b) Young mothers could find a source of informal advice, sharing of experience and short term baby sitting in "kaffeeklatsch" centers near marketing and public service areas. Social agencies might contribute through experimentation with new forms. (c) Social workers could serve as intermediaries between craft and hobby programs and potential users of the products. An example of this kind of activity is a toy lending service which I observed in a Danish housing development where the older people not only do the construction and repair of toys but also operate the service.

COMPREHENSIVE NEIGHBORHOOD MOBILIZATIONS

Such programs as Mobilization for Youth and Haryou in New York City, and similar programs in many major American cities, launched the "new look" in the current American approach to social problems. Initially they were antidelinquency in purpose but later they became the core of an antipoverty urban community development movement. The path of conceptualization in the development of these programs has been from "delinquency treatment" to "delinquency prevention" to "youth development" and finally to the "opening of opportunity." [6] At the level of initial planning (but perhaps never fully implemented) the major focus was on preventive services rather than the traditional social welfare programs: increasing participation of people in seeking solutions to local problems; encouraging indigenous leadership; opening local occupational and educational opportunities to youth and offering the guidance and resources which will permit such opportunities to be exploited; developing new, local, cultural and social resources which reflect the life patterns of local residents. Emphasis also was placed on developing social services that "reach out" to "lower class" people, accepting them on their own terms and finding ways to offer the help they need in a manner most likely to assure its usefulness.

The direct service philosophy of these programs is continuous with social work tendencies since World War II and is best discussed below in the context of such services. Of the other efforts subsumed under the "youth development" and "opening opportunity" banners, it must be said (because this too often is forgotten) that while these programs were both new and radical when contrasted with the clinical social work of the 1950s and also dependent on the influx of social scientists and other professionals, *they derived their central community development conception and methodology from social work*. Their value system reflected the social work value system. The social work profession has responded with enthusiasm to these experimental programs and there is every reason to believe that, if the considerable investment of funds begins to show results, a change process will be well under way which will affect greatly social work education and all social work activities. In fact, some change in the profession has already occurred on the basis of conviction and promise alone, at a time too early to gauge the concrete achievements of the experimental programs.

KNOWLEDGE AND PLANNING

The early settlement pioneers moved into the urban slums determined, among other things, to report to their fellows on "how the other half lives." Some of the workers in the Association for the Improvement of the Conditions of the Poor (late 1840s) and the Charity Organization Societies (1880s) had a similar goal. Some did report. Some still do. Their efforts have been supplemented in recent years, however, by the more systematic social research efforts of social scientists and social workers. This "sharing of knowledge" is potentially a fundamentally important contribution of social work to the improvement of the urban environment.

First, because of their skills in case services social workers are in a position to help people relate and compare their experience with those of others. The need for guidelines in this area is great since one's self-image as parent, worker, mate, or citizen is shaped in a constant process of interaction and self-evaluation. Urban isolation or stratification often deprives individuals of base line data, so to speak. More emphasis might be placed therefore on having social workers conduct, plan and provide information for, or prepare publications for, various types of courses and other "extension efforts" for parents (and teachers, policemen, housing managers, and others). The exact form of the contribution would vary with the setting, but some experience has already been gained, many more possibilities are open in the areas of adult education, mental health courses, health education efforts, child guidance courses for parents, teacher alertness courses, and so on.

Second is a potentially large and very significant contribution by social work to social planning and policy. This broad area can be discussed here only very briefly, but one aspect is particularly relevant. Those who would rebuild or rehabilitate slum areas, end discrimination, open new pathways to people who have suffered deprivation, or develop new ways to cope with local problems, need a much greater understanding of the underlying "culture" of the population which is to be affected. Herbert Gans has charged that in one situation which he observed, social workers failed to have such understanding.[7] I do not know whether he is right in this instance, but social workers certainly have failed periodically in this regard. On the other hand, the history of social work, particularly in the settlements and at certain periods in the family agencies, has been by and large a history of perceptive understanding and reporting of the lives of the dispossessed. Bremner credits social work with a major contribution to the discovery of poverty.[8] I hope that it will make a real and accurate contribution, through the reporting of experience and research, to the developing debate as to whether the goal of services in lower class areas should be: (a) to offer services responsible to and appreciative of people's backgrounds, situations, education—but *premised on equipping people for upward mobility* (as I would argue), or (b) to seek ways of socially legitimating and stabilizing lower class "life styles" that have value premises and social functions which are at variance with middle-class culture (and in the process, perhaps, fail to equip the lower-class citizen with the ability to grasp the opportunities in the broader society).

It is to be expected that the now much valued and needed social work activity which draws on its knowledge of the everyday lives of people will continue and indeed grow in importance. A settlement house's reports of its neighbors' problems with the cost of prescription drugs was an important element in launching a series of events which eventually led to the Senate drug inquiry, for example.

In another area, social work is beginning to make an important contribution to understanding the problems, needs, priorities of those persons who are affected by city planning. This contribution has been formalized in the employment of social workers in urban renewal, city planning, and neighborhood conservation agencies. It might be noted that American sociologists are making a significant bid for a similar role, whereas in the past—unlike their British colleagues—they have not usually oriented their research to problems of social policy. Since social work and sociology do have somewhat different perspectives on human experience, and different ways of assembling social data, one could express the hope that housing, urban renewal, city planning, and neighborhood conservation efforts would find ways usefully to tap the contributions of each. Social work faces the necessity of considerable curricular and field work change in most of its graduate programs, however, if it wishes more than very few of its graduates to find their way into such activities.

Even more will have to be done within social work education, research, and practice before a significant number of social workers are equipped adequately for high level staff and leadership roles in broader social policy and planning efforts. It is difficult to know how large a commitment the profession will be willing to make in this direction at a time when it is hard-pressed to meet its direct-service obligations, though the pressures for such a commitment are growing rapidly.

CASE SERVICES IN A NEW PERSPECTIVE

The discussion thus far in this essay has focused primarily on the present modest but potentially increasing contribution of social work to the areas of social change, social policy and planning, and new social provision. These are the important new areas which require much greater emphasis and development in the profession. Beyond this, of course—or, more accurately, even before this—we must turn to the question of what social work may or should do in its direct-service activities better to serve the disadvantaged, handicapped, and casualties of urban life.

Adequate discussion would require several volumes. A basic approach may be suggested, however, through brief comments under the headings which follow:

1. *The need to increase the amount of service available.* Little else makes sense unless there are enough services. Whatever the rationalizations, long waiting lists cannot be justified and token demonstration projects solve few problems. Basic counseling, guidance, protective, rehabilitative, and supportive social services must be sufficient in number, well distributed, adequately diversified, and staffed by competent personnel. This is fundamental and it cannot be achieved without larger financial commitment,

expanded training, more public acceptance and demand, and internal reforms of the kinds suggested below.

2. *The development of social services and financial assistance as a "right."* Case services at present are not developed on the needed scale, are not used by some segments of the population where they are needed, and are blocked in their impact on many clients because of a not inconsiderable "poor law" residue. The story is an old one and needs little repetition here. The request for relief or counseling too often is taken as evidence of personal moral inadequacy or inferiority. Yet, modern society has ample evidence of the fact that personal problems and financial need are often the product of social forces over which the individual cannot prevail. The available knowledge about personality and interpersonal difficulties seems adequate enough to warrant the same acceptance of emotional and relationship difficulties that society gives to physical illness. There is still a long way to go in gaining general acceptance of this view, however.

Related to the educational and "reporting of the facts" roles mentioned above, one must stress the social work profession's obligation to conceptualize and organize the assistances and social services in ways which are consistent with our present understanding of etiology and with the constant need for vigilance against "poor law" survivals. Public assistance for those in need is constantly reaffirmed by social workers as a *moral* right, but so far it is only in part a *legal* right. Social workers have an obligation to support income maintenance reform, an innovation that is designed to assure, as a matter of right and without consequent stigma and disability, that those without enough money for many different reasons are enabled to achieve a minimum standard of health and decency through transfer payments. Predictable risks and statuses can be covered on an insurance basis; others through legally guaranteed assistance. Social service case evaluation in assistance programs sometimes becomes moral judgment, so it is necessary to consider as part of this reform the administrative relationship between income maintenance and social services.

At the same time, counseling, guidance and therapeutic programs need to be housed, located, defined, organized, and conducted fully to protect the dignity of users and to combat the self or social definition of users as outcasts. Close scrutiny of what actually occurs discloses much that might be done.

3. *The relation of social services to goals and tasks.* I have written elsewhere about the implications of the fact that social services are publicly supported to achieve certain objectives, and these services should be held accountable for their accomplishments. Too often, expressed satisfaction with the goal and with elements of the service process are substituted for the more important concern with results.

A modern social services network must constantly reexamine its professional goals, with the participation of both citizens and professionals, and it should develop better mechanisms for proper coordination, case integration and the measurement of effectiveness.[9] Most people in serious difficulty can be helped only by a well-integrated system of services, competently staffed. Distinctions between public and voluntary agencies, separations among the several sectarian programs, or the allocation of responsibility to the several levels of government, all have their rationales and historical explanations. But these do not excuse the recurring situations in which individual agencies operate as though they were independent entrepeneurs in an eighteenth century market economy.

Progress is being made in translating into organizational realities the conviction as to the need for an accountable, integrated services network. Each locale must make its contribution to such a formulation and adopt methods suitable to its situation. Social work direct-service practitioners would do well to ask themselves if they are not sometimes overinfluenced by the model of the private specialist in medicine, while ignoring the potential of the public health pattern.

4. *The need for new service models.* Administrative reform will not be enough if the intervention modes which are employed are not themselves constantly being improved. A more complete understanding of social work clientele, based on the incorporation of social science insights together with a realistic assessment of what does and does not achieve results, has already pointed toward and in some cases instigated important reforms in social work services: family diagnosis and treatment; new group

method; efforts to intervene into a total institutional milieu; new respect for "concrete services," where once only intrapsychic therapy was valued; new respect for advice and guidance as helpful to people, where once personality change was the only respected goal; increased emphasis on keeping people in the community during the process of rehabilitation, thus simplifying the task, and so on. In addition, new insights from organizational theory have suggested ways in which the organizational setting can be improved so as to maximize the effectiveness of the service.

While the list is long, the lessons are only in part derived and much is yet to be understood and applied. I believe that significant beginnings have been made, that competent people have taken on the task, and that much more may be expected. If all of this can be carried out with an alertness to defects in the individual's milieu, so that concrete services are given as needed but broader environmental reform is addressed where more appropriate, there is every reason to believe that social services will become more acceptable *and* more potent.

CONCLUSIONS

The narrow application of the criteria of the marketplace alone probably would not make the case for the institutional innovations and reforms in social service here outlined. It is only when one introduces broader concerns and refers to other basic values that one derives the goals and requirements of a full attack on the social inadequacies of life in urban-industrial communities. The elements in the resulting new balance sheet were not known to early students of the market. They are nonetheless fundamental to a society whose basic quality depends on new commitments to welfare. Because of this, the challenges for social work discussed in this essay assume considerable urgency and priority. The profession's record in the past provides a basis for the hope that the response will be adequate.

NOTES

1. See Alfred J. Kahn, editor, *Issues in American Social Work* (New York: Columbia University Press, 1959), 3–38.
2. Harold L. Wilensky and Charles N. Lebeaux, *Industrial Society and Social Welfare* (New York: Russell Sage Foundation, 1958), pp. 138–147.

3. Alfred J. Kahn, "Therapy, Prevention and Developmental Provision: A Social Work Strategy," in *Public Health Concepts in Social Work Education* (New York: Council on Social Work Education, 1962). Or "Social Services as Social Utilities" in *Urban Development,* Proceedings XIIIth International Conference of Social Work (New York: Columbia University Press, 1967).
4. *Ibid.*
5. From Alfred J. Kahn, *Planning Community Services for Children in Trouble* (New York: Columbia University Press, 1963), pp. 141–143. Also see Alfred J. Kahn, et al., *Neighborhood Information Centers* (New York: Columbia University School of Social Work, 1966).
6. See Alfred J. Kahn, "From Delinquency Treatment & Community Development" in P. Lazarsfeld, H. Wilensky and W. Sewell, editors, *The Uses of Sociology* (New York: Basic Books, 1967).
7. Herbert Gans, "The Settlement House and the Attack on Urban Poverty," based on a paper presented May, 1963, mimeographed. Also, *The Urban Villagers* (New York: The Free Press, 1962).
8. Robert Bremner, *From the Depths* (New York: New York University Press, 1956).
9. See Alfred Kahn, *Planning Community Services for Children in Trouble* (New York: Columbia University Press, 1963).

# 5 Government, the Arts, and the City

**August Heckscher**

The Arts and the City: it is late to argue that the arts are good for man, giving him much of such pleasure and zest as he derives from his pilgrimage on this small planet. But it is not too late, perhaps, to say something significant upon the importance of the arts to the vitality and health of the city.

It is true that the arts have not formed, so far as I know, the cause and starting point of any great modern city. Men came together first for trade or manufacture, or defense, or for the changing (as at a riverhead or seaport) of the means of transportation which they had been using. Cities also have been formed—for example, Washington or Brazilia—to be governing centers; or to be centers of worship or centers of learning. But to every city that has counted for something, the arts have been added. And today this plus, this final touch of joy and grace, seems to be becoming one of the city's chief supports and a principal underpinning.

In the literature put out by chambers of commerce across the country, the presence of a good symphony and theatre company, of libraries and parks, is given almost as high a priority as a good water supply and ample labor resources. One must presume that the heads of these chambers of commerce, these eminently worldly and practical men, know what they are talking about.

The reason the arts have become important in attracting new industry is that the nature of the work force has been changing in this post-industrial age. The nature of work itself has been changing. The worker increasingly wears a white collar instead of a blue; he is engaged in services rather than the production of goods; he is more educated—and his wife as well. His children have expectations beyond anything in the minds of an earlier generation.

In New York we worry a good deal about the future. Everyone is jumpy if a few corporations move out to the suburbs. But the future of the greatest of all cities seems to me safe just so long as the preeminence of its cultural institutions is assured. I do not mean only such formal manifestations of art as the museums, the opera, the ballet, the symphony. I mean, as well, the whole sparkling and colorful life that clusters around the making of art and fashion—the critics, the journals, the clubs and cafés, the shops and galleries, the streets alive with jostling people, the parks with their own kind of delights and surprises. And of course the artists themselves, the creative individuals whose spell extends far beyond the walls of their studios, studies, or workshops.

Looking ahead, it seems clear that when other considerations no longer compel men to gather closely in cities, the arts will continue to provide an irresistible attraction and bond. Today manufacturing *can* be done in the city; it is important that a certain amount of it should be done there. But it is no longer essential from the point of view of the manufacturer himself. He is far less dependent than formerly upon being close to a particular source of raw material; his labor supply, far from being exclusively centered in the city, has to be brought in from suburban distances. The speed of transportation and communication gives the manufacturer a large freedom to settle where he wills. This is now becoming equally true of management, with its army of clerks and office workers. The boss can communicate with his secretary, and retrieve information, over distances and through decentralized channels.

What makes men want to gather in cities, once technology has removed the necessity of their doing so, is partly such a simple, age-old thing as a liking for companionship and gossip. But it is also—and perhaps chiefly—a delight in the amenities which the city alone provides. These include the color and variety of life on the street, the unexpectedness with which things are always happening—the chance encounter and the "strange and fatal" interview. They include as well the great theatres and museums and scientific and horticultural displays:

in brief, the whole cultural life of the place. These become the *raison d'être* for the central city when older necessities have vanished or been weakened. They make it seem worthwhile to put up with such things as crowding and waiting, and the taxi that doesn't appear on a rainy night, and even the subway with its unholy torments.

It may be asked whether the cultural life, too, cannot be decentralized. Within limits I believe it can, and that it is an obligation upon us to see that this is done. The arts should be brought out of their ancient, exclusive citadels, and be made mobile like so much else that is characteristic of our civilization. I have the hope for New York that we shall be able to establish through the five boroughs companies for touring and for exchange, with cultural centers smaller and more modest than that on Lincoln Square providing nearby pleasures for the people. Beyond that, the suburbs in the next decade or two will surely establish cultural institutions of their own.

Yet in the last analysis, it is the nature of art to require the vitality of numbers and an almost exaggerated intensity of life. The great public, the great audience, is essential to the creative spirit. There may in time be many centers, comparable to that which now casts its dazzling glow from the heart of Manhattan. But centers in the real sense they must be: diffusion and sprawl are fatal to the development of a rich artistic life.

Let us now ask what the city has been doing to foster the arts. The short answer might seem to be that it has been doing surprisingly little. In Europe the principal of municipal assistance to the theatre, opera, and ballet has been long established. Royal collections, once the exclusive property of a small group, have been democratized and made available to the people with subsidies providing for their maintenance and enhancement. But the conventional wisdom in the United States has decreed that cultural institutions shall be private, and shall, so long as possible, resist the encroachments of a wicked and meddling government.

The conventional wisdom is not, of course, always honored. A survey made in the 1950s by the Library of Congress showed such cities as Atlanta, Georgia, and Buffalo, New York, making contributions to such causes as support of the symphony, of open air theatre and pop concerts. Cleveland, Chicago, Philadelphia, and Boston would not be the distinguished centers for art they are today had public funds not been made available to their major cultural institutions.

On the West Coast the principle of municipal support to arts is now well established. A politician running for office in California, Professor Mel Scott has told us in a scholarly monograph, "would risk defeat if he opposed assistance to the community symphony orchestra or an adequate appropriation for the cultural programs of the recreation department."

Nevertheless public aid to the arts, once it became a matter of serious concern in the United States, was focused principally at the federal and state levels, rather than the municipal. This is, I presume, because the cities have been poor, and also because they have, for the most part, been poorly and unimaginatively governed.

Thus the National Foundation for the Arts has had in principle some $10 million to dispense annually in support of the arts. Of this it gives up to $50,000 in matching funds to each state that sets up an Arts Council. The State Arts Council movement, partly a result of this spur, has been quite remarkable in its development. Today all the fifty states, as well as a few odd American territories, are thus culturally equipped. But even before the federal government was making its small matching grant available, New York under Governor Nelson Rockefeller had pioneered effectively. Appropriations by the legislature have given it sums to spend annually which not long ago were approximately half a million dollars, and soon may reach $2 million. These amounts have been dispersed to bring the arts to communities which have been regularly bypassed. At the same time they have helped support the budgets of the companies and institutions whose services were being engaged.

Meanwhile, however, the cities lagged. San Francisco has had a 3 percent hotel tax, the proceeds being spent for cultural and recreational events which hopefully would bring more tourists to the city. The promotion of culture under this head and for these purposes has not been altogether a success. Other cities have had arts councils composed of citizens acting on their own and without city support. Recently I participated in a survey made by Chicagoans of their cultural resources, resulting in strong recommendations that such obvious deficiencies in the cultural life as the lack of a repertory theatre or a museum of modern art be rectified by concerted action, and that an Arts Council, suitably staffed and financed, be set up.

Perhaps the cities that have done most for the arts so far have done it as a result of dynamic if intermittent political leadership. One thinks of New York's La Guardia, whose interest could penetrate to every corner of the city's life—from hot dogs to Haydn—and who never failed to see the city as something more than a physical entity. One thinks of more recent mayors in other cities, like William Hartsfield of Atlanta and Charles Farnsley of Louisville. Mr. Farnsley once told me that as mayor he acted on the principle that "when he could save a dollar on roads and sewers it went into the library or some such institution." He personally organized the Louisville Fund, one of the most successful examples of a united fund-raising system for support of the arts.

Mr. Hartsfield, when you talk with him, professes to be chary of organized public ways of helping the arts; yet few men have done as much as he to bring liveliness and distinction to an American city. He will explain with a twinkle in his eye how within existing arrangement he can find means enough for supporting the arts. Everything from the use of municipal posters to municipal parking lots, from the police power to the recreation authorities, he would put to work to give Atlanta a more lively cultural environment.

Space does not permit me to develop in this brief essay the exciting and important contributions which have been made to the arts by the John Lindsay administration in New York City. There is no question that Mayor Lindsay came to his present office with the conviction that the arts are one of New York's crucial assets, and that everything which can be done to support and stimulate them serves directly the city's interest. This conviction was demonstrated vividly by the appointment of Tom Hoving as his first Recreation and Cultural Affairs Administrator, a new position which the mayor established early in his administration. This is the job that I later inherited.

Hoving was a man who had been a curator of one of the city's great museums and who had an instinctive feeling for the cultural delights of this world. Tom Hoving took the parks for his stage, and within them presented a series of sudden, haphazard, and often quite dazzling performances. Of course the parks had been used for music and entertainment before, but not with the same *élan*. And certainly not with the same response from the people.

Next I turn to a broad range of matters on which I can also touch but briefly: they may be summed up under the phrase, The Art of the City. For any municipality that today concerns itself with the arts must take into account the quality of the environment. Here I distinguish two approaches: (1) Architecture as one of the arts which needs to be promoted and preserved; (2) The city as a home for the arts—one which either supports or undermines them.

First, the city itself as an art form, the container of such works of art as beautiful buildings, squares, statues, monuments, fountains, parks. It is as important for the city to develop and maintain standards in these objects, as it is in such other forms as dancing, music, and the theatre. A city that fully recognizes its responsibility to the visual and performing arts will not neglect to act in the environmental arts.

In an earlier period cities aimed at a high level of excellence in their public buildings. Through the twenties a certain grandeur, even if derivative and false, characterized most civic architecture. By the late forties it seemed good to break away from outmoded forms—the pillars that no longer played a structural role, the ornamentation added superficially. Many of us rejoiced to see the more honest and functional contemporary style replace a sham classicism or renaissance style. But soon we observed uneasily that the contemporary often was an excuse for shoddiness and bareness—buildings without scale or variety or texture. A battle for honesty had been won; but the fruits of victory were lost in a new streak of economy and commonplace meanness.

At the same time, through a period of depression, war, and cold war, other aspects of the city declined in visual appeal. Parks and public squares were neglected and were allowed to be encroached upon by a savage commercialism. Public services, like subways and railroad stations, became increasingly shoddy. Many of the structures of an earlier day, still possessing a faded charm and often capable of being filled with new life, were ruthlessly torn down. Even the trees in the streets were destroyed, as the traffic rights of way were widened and the automobile was given complete sovereignty over all other values within the cityscape.

The cycle has once more turned, and signs are discernible of a public concern for the aesthetic quality of all that the city constructs and has care of. I would not say that we are again in a golden age. It is extremely difficult to argue, within the broken-down economics of our cities, for the spending of money for beauty's sake alone. Yet sometimes through the farseeing courage of city officials, and sometimes as a result of aid from the private sector and the federal government, the cities are able to do good and gracious things: to plant flowers and trees; to set out new fountains, to light the buildings delicately at night, to preserve the old when it would seem easier and cheaper to destroy it, and above all to create buildings with a fresh richness and elegance, set forth in the idiom of their own times.

The best architects are today being brought into the service of the cities. The national competition held for the design of the new city hall of Boston was a sign that tradition or mediocrity could be exorcised from great public works. In New York City today there is hardly an architect of major renown who has not been called upon to contribute his talents to the design of the city—and most of them, I am proud to say, are working on the landscaping and the structures of the parks. Schools are beginning to look less dreary and monotonous; even housing has begun to get away from the chilling inhumanity which has become its hallmark.

In this field, as in support of the other arts, the determination and taste of the city's political leadership becomes absolutely crucial. Without that, even the most enlightened men in the city's departments and agencies are not able to act effectively on behalf of good design. But even with such leadership, certain institutions can play important roles in promoting overall quality in the objects and places of the city. I shall mention three organizations of a public nature; I need hardly add that these in turn will be effective only as they are supported by a citizenry that cares for beauty and by many voluntary organizations that give backing—and often unsought-for advice—to the city authorities.

In New York the first and most venerable of the official bodies charged with maintaining excellence in the public sphere is the

Art Commission. This has the responsibility for reviewing all public buildings, street furniture, signs, monuments, etc., built or erected by the city. It can veto; and its veto can occasionally be effective in stopping a patently bad building or monument. But the fact that its veto can be overridden makes it chary of using this power. Moreover it waits until a project is presented to it, at a stage when the architect has been chosen and a veto would only result in a new choice almost as bad as the first. In the past the Art Commission has been dominated by traditional views of art and architecture; but recent appointments under John Lindsay assure that contemporary tastes will at last be forcibly represented.

A second official body is concerned not with overseeing change but with resisting it: this is the recently established New York City Landmarks Commission. It is still too early to tell how effectively this will work; moreover by the time it began to get going, a very large number of New York landmarks had already fallen under the wrecker's ball. The difficulty facing this commission is that the attachment of the status of landmark to one's property inevitably reduces its economic value. People can hardly be blamed for resisting the satisfaction of living in an historic house, if they know they will be severely penalized if they try to sell it. A tax concession on such real estate would be the obviously effective means of making architectural conservation a practical measure. I hope we shall see this effectuated.

A third such official body in New York was recommended by the recent Paley Report on the design of the city. This is a small Council on Urban Design, which is the Mayor's vigilant and imaginative advisor on all matters relating to architecture and civic design. It is in part an "early warning system," making sure that public works do not get started without foreknowledge and a chance to judge them in terms of their effect on the cityscape. It will also spark the use of new talent and the development of imaginative approaches, and is charged in general with concern for the city's visual aspect and its artistically harmonious development.

The conception of the Council on Urban Design leads us into a larger and more subtle aspect of the city as a work of art. Not only must it be filled with well-designed objects and places, but it must present an aesthetically pleasing form, with its parts sympathetically related to each other and its various functions visually defined. The Paley Report speaks in a telling phrase of the "oppressive endlessness" of much of the New York scene— and it may be said as truly of most American cities. To stop the eye, to create open spaces and enclosures in successive and often surprising contrasts; to shape *places* where there is now too often a blurred and ambiguous *placelessness:* that is the highest art of civic design.

The city contains within itself the powers to shape the scene as an artist in any medium would shape his material and give form to his vision. The creation of open spaces is a vital tool; and there is every reason why parks should be conceived both for their recreational functions and also for their role in giving form to the urban landscape. Squares and avenues play the same form-giving role. Public Transport provides further leverage. I recall in San Francisco, when the new subway system was still being viewed boldly and imaginatively, one of the men working on it said to me: "We are not shaping a transportation system; we are shaping a city."

Think what a framework is made when a subway opens pleasingly on a well-proportioned and landscaped square. Thereafter cumulative decisions by public and private interests can be counted on to fill in the picture and to make a new and memorable place within the city.

Finally there is something to be said about the city as an appropriate environment for the arts—all the arts—visual, performing, architectural. Great ballet or theatre will not fare well if no one can approach the theatre because of the traffic; music in the parks will not delight the summer evening if planes are flying low overhead; even good architecture will not count if the air is so polluted that the buildings' outlines are but dimly perceived. In short, the city has a responsibility for removing those negative factors which frustrate the life of the arts.

More than that: the city that really cares for the arts will try to create a general setting in which they can be easily appreciated and enjoyed. This seems like an obvious point. But it is in fact overlooked. If the United States fails to reach the level of art which now seems to be within the reach of its artists and creators, it may well be for reasons that have nothing to do with art itself, or even with such subtle sociological factors as the growth of mass culture or the stress on technological values. It may simply be because the city—which is the only place where art can really thrive—has lost little by little the capacity to provide a fit home for the arts.

So simple and elementary a thing as the lack of housing for artists could cause the decline of a city's fame. Its institutions might be well supported by private and public patronage; its creative spirit could be continually fed by the strange waters of artistic genius. Yet if there were no old lofts in the city where the artists could live and work, no studios where they could toil with ample space and light and at rents they can afford, then all else could avail little.

To be involved in the government of a city can be a dreary business; it can also be one of the most challenging of all tasks today, one of the most exciting and rewarding. The ultimate reward will come only to those who realize that what they govern is no humdrum place, but alive with the possibilities of the spirit and containing within itself creative energies waiting to be released. And the highest expression of this spirit is through the arts—the high arts as seen on the stage or in the museum, and the popular arts as heard in singing voices in a park at evening or in play that reaches toward something more than play.

Such arts crown the city. They justify its existence. They shed upon all who serve it with zest and imagination a light which lightens even the humblest task.

# 6 The Church and the Urban Condition

David Popenoe

THE URBAN CONDITION

Seventy percent of the people in our nation now live in what the U.S. Census defines as urban places, and 65 percent live in metropolitan areas. By 1985 some 85 percent of our population will be living in metropolitan areas, and almost all will be living in urban places of one kind or another. While the population shift from rural to urban has taken place for the most part since the turn of the century, the rate of movement is declining because there are less and less rural people left to migrate to the cities. In a mostly urban nation classical urbanization no longer describes the principal processes with which we should be concerned. It is not the shift from rural to urban but the development and changes within metropolitan areas that should command our attention. We are a highly urbanized nation, but precisely what does this mean in terms of community patterns within urbanized areas?

Large cities, which dominated in our industrializing period, are in economic and social decline across the nation when compared to the suburbs which surround them. The larger the city, the greater the relative population decline—and certain very large cities have undergone an absolute population decline. Population decline is usually associated with a decline in economic, social, and cultural vitality, and in the quality of physical facilities. More importantly, this population decline has been selective—only the middle- and upper-income whites have moved out—and even where center city populations have stabilized in numbers or even increased, there has been a dramatic change in the character of this population. Middle-income whites have been and are continuing to be replaced by low-income nonwhites. Thus the leadership and much of the economic vitality associated with middle- and upper-income groups are now found predominantly in the suburbs, and the social and economic problems associated with low-income groups, particularly those that are discriminated against, have come to dominate central city life. This has created a situation where the traditional roles of center city and suburbia are reversed. It is the city which is now *sub*-urban, that is, dependent on the so-called suburbs, rather than vice versa.

The suburbs are by no means without their problems, but these are problems of too rapid growth rather than decline. And because suburbs are typically small, fractionated, and often specialized communities, they are often, like the central cities, without the means and resources to achieve solutions. They are very much dependent on other suburbs and still in large degree, of course, on the central cities.

In a general sense, the metropolis can be viewed as a complex system consisting of a number of specialized parts (communities, organizations, jobs, workers, and so on) each of which is dependent upon most of the others for getting its needs met and its problems solved. In this and many other respects it is a microcosm of the conditions that prevail generally in our society.

Urbanization as a broad social reality is basically a matter of the increasing specialization, interdependence, and complexity of life. Thus, occupational specialization has increased markedly in the period of urbanization, land uses have become more segregated in space, and so on, and each unit in the structure of society, because it is more specialized, is more dependent on every other unit—whether these units are people, communities or formal human groupings of one type or another (*e.g.*, businesses, churches, schools, families). Since these units *are* increasingly interdependent, it is particularly important that they be aware of the fact, that they be in communication, and that they serve the interests of one another in a mutually rewarding manner.

The family situation can be used as an analogy. We know that children are greatly dependent on their parents, and the parents on each other, for meeting a wide variety of the individual needs of each. What happens when these dependent statuses are not fully realized by each individual, when there is a breakdown in communication, or when one party simply does not want to cooperate with the others? These conditions lead to family breakdown which injures all parties. This breakdown can sometimes occur through the triggering effect of the malfunctioning of only a single relationship, for example between parent and child.

Most of what we call urban or metropolitan problems are similarly the result of some kind of breakdown in the relationship between two interdependent units, or in some cases the complete lack of any formal relationship at all. Suburbs and central cities are all dependent upon one another, but the lack of adequate transportation networks, the fractionization of governmental units, and the clash of social class and racially based patterns of value combine to prevent the establishment of efficient working relationships. The poor are dependent upon others for the education needed to secure a decent job, and for the availability of jobs once they have received a certain education, yet the relationships in the metropolitan system are not always such as to provide either the education or the jobs in the necessary quantity and quality.

For the same reasons of complexity and interdependence, a social problem more quickly becomes a burden to the entire community. When an industry pollutes a stream, the deleterious effects are quickly felt downstream; when a pathological environment generates a large number of criminals, the crimes are committed over ever-larger areas; when the central cities suffer an economic decline, the suburbs are by no means isolated from the effects; when the roadside landscape is mutilated, it is seen by thousands of passers-by; when the Negro is discriminated against in the South, the whole nation suffers the consequences of the urban condition.

It was not always this way. In our rural past, communities were isolated and not dependent upon one another. Farmers were not necessarily dependent upon others for jobs, for food, and for many of the things in their daily lives. What happened in another part of the world was not a national problem.

CAUSES AND SOLUTIONS

If any single factor can be said to account for our present complex and interdependent situation, it is technological development. It is the same factor that primarily accounts for the rise of large cities and for our high material standard of living. The only way to turn back the clock is to decide to stop using our technological achievements—to return to a greater use of human as opposed to nonhuman sources of energy. Since this would mean giving up our material standard of living, as well as giving up our cities, it is a decision that most people would not voluntarily make. A few persons *have* chosen to go back to the land—to a self-sufficient farming and handicraft economy. But these actions do nothing to solve the problems that remain for the rest of us.

We must therefore deal with our *present* society as best we can, and within the rules of the game which almost everyone seems to want to play. The urban problems which plague our nation must be solved by better relating the interdependent units of urban areas and of society with one another. This means, in general, that many of our contemporary social problems cannot be solved except through a greater "rationalization" of the many relationships and dependencies that exist in our society. It is essentially this process which has been used by our large business and industrial corporations—the most successful units of modern society by most people's standards. It means, if we are to follow the corporation's analogy, that there may have to be even more specialization of parts, a greater amount of centralized and comprehensive planning, coordination and control, a better established hierarchy of authority, and the increased formalization and "prescription" of relationships. These are the organizational elements that have led to great technical efficiency in economic production. They are almost certainly the elements that could lead to greater efficiency in the social sector, in terms of more efficient exchanges between those persons and groups who have needs and those who have the resources to meet those needs.

In short, if our urban areas were run with the procedures and the efficiency of large corporations, we could solve many of our urban problems in short order. There are innumerable hurdles to overcome in the pursuit of such efficiency, of course, such as certain traditional values, vested interests, and inertia, but the general tendency is toward jumping over these hurdles in one way or another. Think what would happen if the government's "outer space" program were instead the "urban space" program! Major breakthroughs would come in a very few years, and many of our present urban problems could probably be solved in ten to twenty years.

## SOME CONSEQUENCES

Grave dangers undoubtedly lie in store for society if our urban problems—in such fields as poverty, education, housing, pollution, water supply, physical rejuvenation of blighted areas, transportation, crime, racial relations, and so on—are not solved. Few maintain, therefore, that we should make no attempt toward their solution. The disagreements arise over the means of solution. I would hold that any solution which does not involve a somewhat greater rationalization of society, as explained above, will not get the job done. Because of the American's penchant for success, therefore, I predict that we will live to see a more highly rationalized society than we have today. This raises a new set of problems, however, which are beginning to be seen today but which may be far more visible and pernicious in the future. These are problems that may be the not so beneficent consequences of a high degree of rationalization of our social life, and they are of two general types: effects on democracy as a system of values and political behavior, and effects on the individual personality.

First, a corporation is not run democratically. Could a city or society be run like a corporation and still preserve democracy? The answer is probably not. Cities and societies will have to engage in much more give and take, in less centralized planning, and in weaker lines of authority if freedom and individual participation are to be preserved. This is not to say, however, that cities and the society could not be far more efficient than they now are and still protect the democratic ethos.

The second danger of the general trend toward rationalization, and the one which I want to emphasize in this paper, is its impact on the individual. It is by no means certain that an individual living his life in a "corporate environment" can achieve full human development. The overrationalized environment may be to some extent dehumanizing, that is lacking in deep emotional content, in individuality, and in warm human relationships. A good many contemporary social critics strongly hold this belief. If true, it means that increasingly we may have to preserve "bastions of intimacy" in the large-scale, rationalized society so that persons can spend at least part of their lives, particularly their early lives, in environments that have the characteristics of the family, the neighborhood, and the small community—so-called primary or face-to-face groups.

### THE SOCIAL ROLE OF THE CHURCH

The general trend toward a more rationalized society is almost certainly going to be spearheaded during the coming years by the national government, which has become by far the most important institution in our society. Since the government increasingly dominates (not necessarily in an authoritarian way) the major institutions of our society—business, industry, agriculture, the professions, science, education, and so on, it seems reasonable to suppose that these institutions will be increasingly aligned with the government in its overall mission. One major institution is an exception, however—the church. By law and by custom, the church remains outside the institutional hierarchy that has the national government at its apex. This fact has by no means fostered the church's objective importance in modern times— quite the opposite—but it does suggest guidelines for the appropriate social role of the church in our society. Further, the church remains one of the few major institutions in modern society primarily engaged in fostering and actively promoting the moral values of the Judeo-Christian tradition. The hands of most other societal institutions are tied, primarily through specialized function, to a concern with the "technical" side of life. This seems increasingly true even in the area of education. The church, in other words, affects people's hearts whereas almost all other major institutions affect only their heads, their bodies, or their pocketbooks.

In my opinion the social role of the church in modern society has become of critical importance, in spite of (or maybe because of) the trend toward secularization. Increased rationalization has brought increased secularization, that is, a waning of the influence over our daily lives which the church has vis-à-vis other institutions in society. Nevertheless, it is widely agreed that the church has played a central role in the civil rights struggle, and is beginning to play an equally central role in the war on poverty. Its role in these areas is of particular importance because it stands almost alone among major social institutions in the ability to change the hearts and not just the minds of the stable middle-class elements of our society who very often hold the balance of moral and political power and who, of course, are the church's major constituents.

The church has traditionally concentrated on changing society through changing the individual. In contemporary times, more and more social services and social action, including those conducted under religious auspices, are focused on changing the individual through changing society. It is with this orientation that the church is becoming increasingly involved in the major social movements of our time. Since social action is a completely compatible role within the church's broad sense of mission, and because recent events indicate that the church can be a powerful force for good in the social arena, it seems imperative that the church become more deeply engaged in enhancing the efficiency and moral purpose of the public processes that can enrich the lives of all of us. Particular efforts should be directed, it seems to me, toward improving societal efficiency in such a way that opportunities for leading dignified lives can be radically expanded for the nation's "have-nots." But it must be remembered that this cannot be done satisfactorily without the kind of massive application of technical know-how and resources that are presently being utilized for purposes of war production and the conquering of outer space.

In spite of this great need for social action, the church should not forget that its *primary* concern probably still lies in its direct contact with the individual, with the goal not only of individual opportunity but of individual fulfillment. Individual fulfillment may loom ever larger as a problem as it becomes increasingly difficult for the individual to find identity, dignity, and meaning in the face of a possibly depersonalizing environment. Many social critics, philosophers, novelists, theologians, and others have made terms like alienation, loss of identity, anxiety, and meaninglessness into designations of important symptoms of our time. The problems which these conditions pose for individual growth and development are being handled by an increasing variety of "helping professions" whose methods and goals approach ever more closely those of religion, particularly the new existential and humanistic therapies, and by religious counselors whose methods have become more secular. There are many instances today in fact where the content of the minister's therapy is far more secular than the mental health worker's therapy!

Problems of individual growth and development obviously cannot fully be solved by psychotherapy, particularly in the face of evidence that therapy, at least as it presently is practiced, is of only limited value, nor can these problems be solved entirely by specialists in an age when overspecialization is part of the problem. Their occurrence must be *prevented* through the establishment of rich and personalized environments at the more intimate levels of family, neighborhood, church and local community—environments which should be characterized by the kinds of human relationships necessary to the fuller humanization of man.

With the great mobility of modern society, neighborhoods and communities are changed quite frequently. Only the church, and hopefully the family, remain as the base for a set of primary values and relationships that a man can carry with him as he moves from place to place. The church is normally the first place a newcomer to a community turns in search of stable human contact and relationships. This signifies an extremely important social role that the church can play in the urban age—a role which may ultimately overshadow all others in terms of the significance it has for man. The church can become a center for close face-to-face contact in an age where intimate relationships will be at a premium. It can concentrate on the seemingly little things that make life worth living and which give it meaning. It can fill the gaps that education and affluence still leave in our lives. It can help individuals to accomplish the things that the government and the society will never be able to accomplish for them.

In summary, the church's social role in relation to the urban condition can best be brought to focus in the light of the following characteristics of institutional religion in modern urban-industrial society:

(1) It stands relatively apart from the pressures of a centralizing government, and can therefore help to "keep the government honest";

(2) It is the only major institution with a concern for the whole man, including his emotional development;

(3) It operates for the most part at the more intimate level of the local community, and has a set of values and relationships that mobile man can carry with him from place to place;

(4) It is in a unique position to assist in guiding the hearts of the middle and upper classes toward assuring the development of a society of equal opportunity and human dignity for all.

GOALS AND STRATEGIES

The following social goals strike me as being particularly central to the church's mission in urban society:

(1) To promote democratic values in every area of society against the forces of ignorance, apathy, and hate;

(2) To foster efficiency in society, comparable to that achieved in the private sector, to a level adequate for the solution of our pressing urban problems, particularly the problems of the economically and culturally deprived;

(3) To spearhead the creation of true human communities within megalopolis where love, creativity and full individual development can flourish in the spirit of human fellowship.

The first of these goals requires the church to speak out; the second demands that it foster social action toward the achievement of democratic values; the third should be its ultimate and long-run goal—a goal which the state and its agents, no matter how beneficent, will not fully be able to achieve.

One can only hint, in this brief essay, at what some of the more significant strategies might be for the church in the urban age:

(1) Theological symbols and forms will have to change if the church is to attract, as it must, the idealistic youth of the rising generation. Many members of the "new left," for example, have stated that their "ultimate concern" is the establishment of a greater sense of human community and fellowship through which their individual growth and development can best proceed. Yet few of them turn to the church! Rather than seek only to change the older

parishes, the church should probably establish new and experimental groups directed particularly at single persons and young marrieds in the suburbs and the city.

(2) Since a goal of the church is a "ministry of the laity," and because the trend of the times is toward a highly personalized religion in which each person thinks of himself as a minister, the theological establishment should increasingly open itself to the use of lay workers. Theological education, in particular, will have to be drastically revised. The church in its uniqueness may stand counter to the trend that everything is becoming increasingly professionalized. Ministers should increasingly be found in all walks of life; and persons from all walks of life should increasingly perform some of the functions of ministers.

(3) It would be sheer folly, in my estimation, consciously to abandon the neighborhood or parish church as some have proposed. Though the local community may be increasingly unimportant to the male in his world of work, it is by no means unimportant to housewife and child, and to the male as husband and father or in his leisure time. In fact, as we have indicated above, its importance in a certain sphere of life may increase with time. But the parish church may have to undergo some radical changes in form and function. First, it can no longer remain parochial in the derogatory sense of that term. True feelings of human fellowship can best come about through concerted and purposeful action toward goals outside the group, and there are a host of worthwhile goals to strive for. It obviously is impossible to establish a true human community if one's only community interest is his neighbors. The strong family is one which at the same time has great internal unity and cohesion *and* a constant and purposeful flow of relationships outside of itself. The strong parish church is no different. Second, I see no reason why churches should not strive to become "comprehensive voluntary associations" focused primarily on secular things of great value and concern, rather than on trivia. This need not water down the church's essential

spiritual mission, and it distinguishes the church from many other voluntary organizations. Third, the parish churches increasingly may have to become social service centers directed particularly at personal and family problems. But why not? Fourth, the parish churches may have an important role as centers of adult education, at least until such programs become more firmly established under governmental auspices.

(4) The church should continue to explore the possibility of "released time," so that the education of the young is not left entirely in the hands of government-controlled educational institutions which increasingly will be preparing individuals only for "useful roles in society," rather than for full individual growth.

(5) The plight of the inner city parish church, which faces both a declining parish population and a turnover in the character of that population which leads eventually to an entirely low-income ghetto, is tied up, of course, with the general plight of the central cities. Like the city itself, at least in the short run, the inner city church may have to become essentially a welfare station—but one whose major goal is to see that its "clients" are enabled to raise their station in life and probably move to the suburbs. The problems of the inner city church and its surrounding environment should be one of the most important targets of social action on the part of all the churches within the metropolitan area. Most importantly, the suburban churches can help to marshal the leadership and resources needed to achieve social and physical urban renewal of the inner city as a whole. There are too few spokesmen for nonbusiness-oriented goals and strategies in the renewal dialogue at the present time. The morally based goals in urban renewal are by no means as clear cut as they are in civil rights and poverty, but that is another reason why the church's role is critical—it can help to clarify the issues. In addition, the suburban churches have much to do in their own backyards toward removing suburban obstacles to rational and humane metropolitan development.

CONCLUSION

There was a time when the church stood at the center of society. Now its position has been taken by the secular national state. To stay alive the church, like almost every other social structure in modern times, is increasingly going to have to specialize. But specialization is something quite different from decline or decay. And though it may never again be at the center of society, this does not mean that it cannot continue at the center of the individual—as a place for his expression of ultimate concern and commitment in terms which are meaningful in the modern age. Though societies have changed radically through history, there is little indication that the underlying psychological make-up of man has undergone a corresponding transformation. The basic moral insights of the Judeo-Christian tradition seem as valid as they ever were. Justice alone will not bring love, nor will freedom automatically bring individual fulfillment. The efficient society dedicated to human welfare, as badly as we need it, will not be the end of the human endeavor; it may be only the beginning. The focus should shift from social development to individual development. The church, though probably a radically transformed church, has its finest hour still to come.

SELECTED REFERENCES

Angell, Robert Cooley, *Free Society and Moral Crises* (Ann Arbor: University of Michigan Press, 1965).

Boulding, Kenneth, *The Organizational Revolution* (New York: Harper and Brothers, 1953).

Cox, Harvey, *The Secular City* (New York: The Macmillan Co., 1965).

Fromm, Erich, *The Sane Society* (New York: Holt, Rinehart and Winston, 1965).

Greer, Scott, *The Emerging City* (New York: Free Press of Glencoe, 1962).

Haworth, Lawrence, *The Good City* (Bloomington: Indiana University Press, 1963).

Michael, Donald N., *The Next Generation* (New York: Random House, 1963).

Montagu, M. F. Ashley, *The Direction of Human Development* (New York: Harper and Brothers, 1955).

Mowrer, O. Hobert, *The New Group Therapy* (Princeton, New Jersey: D. Van Nostrand and Co., 1964).

Mumford, Lewis, *The Transformations of Man* (New York: Collier Books, 1962).

Nisbet, Robert A., *Community and Power* (New York: Oxford University Press, A Galaxy Book, 1962).

Norton, Perry L., *Church and Metropolis* (New York: The Seabury Press, 1964).

Seidenberg, Roderick, *Anatomy of the Future* (Chapel Hill: University of North Carolina Press, 1961).

Winter, Gibson, *The New Creation as Metropolis* (New York: Macmillan Co., 1963).

# 7 Creative Politics and Urban Citizenship

## Norton E. Long

The political philosophy of Jefferson had a hierarchy of values that is now well nigh reversed. Of paramount importance was the individual, next his local community, next his state, and a poor last the federal union. Jefferson's enthusiasm was largely reserved for the New England town, the only institution that rivaled the state of nature in its attractions. The Jeffersonian order of loyalties has suffered a drastic change. Few besides George Wallace would be torn as was Robert Lee between state and union. Despite the attachment to Robert Wood's "suburban miniature," this attachment amounts in reality to sentimental attitudinizing at best and social absenteeism and escapism at worst. The locus of paramount loyalty is now firmly fixed in the nation, if anywhere. National allegiance is the one allegiance we hesitate to renounce, and the nation is the one institution which can mobilize human and material resources on a major scale. In all else we are civic birds of passage engaged in a shallow politics of limited commitment.

In fact we have gone far toward confusing citizenship with a species of local public goods consumership. The local citizen votes with his feet as he transfers his patronage from some municipal Macy's to some municipal Gimbels. Mayors and city managers resemble so many municipal hotelkeepers competing to attract paying guests and to avoid or shuck the nonpaying variety. Indeed, the exigencies of a fragmented local government in which, in Robert Wood's phrase, "needs are segregated from resources" have produced a set of municipal real estate corporations controlled and motivated by the logic of the property tax rather than any theory of responsible government. In this logic poor citizens are not citizens but in the economic politics of urban renewal so many encumbrances on land destined for a "higher use," to wit for a higher taxpaying use. Solvency of the city is *suprema lex*. In the tax-contrived wonderland of local government municipal nationalism requires the sacrifice of the poor and fiscally unproductive. The municipal corporation like its private enterprise namesake must conserve its assets and ruthlessly shed its liabilities. The political community is not a shared common fate but a limited liability company with little more than a service orientation.

We have assumed that legal citizens would automatically become psychological, ethical, and functional citizens. This assumption is increasingly dubious. Americans have been socialized to the skills of do-it-yourself government. Boorstin's account of the government before government of the wagon train, the claim club, and the mining camp shows that Americans were as ready to play at democratic government as their kids at sand-lot baseball. Also, his report indicates that their commitment was as limited and as temporary. The sovereign individual of Jefferson was coolly ready to up stakes when his interests seemed better served elsewhere. What in Boorstin's story seems a lighthearted versatility admirably suited to the limited needs of a nation on the move on an open frontier is less attractive as a device for dealing with the crowded and complex needs of the modern city. The rugged individualism of the frontier with its habit of mining the soil and moving on is disastrously unconcerned with the preservation of the painfully accumulated social capital of urban life. The sovereign individual going his sovereign way often resembles a Goth in Rome armed with his vote as a battle-axe more inclined to loot and destroy than to preserve and create.

Indeed the theory of consumership and the assimilation of local government and its public goods to a market economy reduces the role of the local citizen to the status of a component of a shifting demand curve and a mobile factor of production. The creation of a national market and with it a nation necessitated the destruction of state and local economic autonomy. A major purpose of the constitution was to quell the incipient mercantilism of the states. The Supreme Court for a considerable part of its history waged war against trade restrictions and only latterly has relaxed its efforts.

The merchant princes of the booster cities of the Midwest were closely tied to the fortunes of local real estate and for a time identified with the economic and political fortunes of their cities. Even here mobility and limited commitment were the rule until a seemingly favorable location induced a major sunk investment. With the declining importance of real estate as a source of wealth, the motivation for burgherlike behavior receded. Corporate civil servants, relating to the national market with a limited local commitment to the preservation of the corporate image through bland participation in welfare and civic ritual, have taken over. Public utility interest in local politics has ebbed, being replaced by routine lobbying. Business concern, except for the plums and public relations of urban renewal, has become fitful and weak in the doings of the city. Officials charged with this aspect of corporate decision making hold minor positions in the corporate hierarchy.

Dahl's investigation of New Haven showed how the early monopoly of a congregational political, business, social elite broke down. First the social elite was replaced in business by a group with different social status, then it was replaced in politics by the new business group, and finally the new business group was replaced by a rising set of ethnic politicians. Thus the hierarchies of social, political, and economic status became split and in different hands. Howard Brotz has pointed to the anomaly that first-class political citizens should be second- or even third-class social and economic citizens and vice versa. This separation of what might be considered different sources of legitimacy amounts to a fragmentation of the resource base whose effective utilization generates political power in Dahl's sense. The bases are ceremonially reunited in the ritual unification of the community for the welfare fund drive and projects such as schools and hospitals. For the most part, the resource bases are exploited at a low rate of utilization corresponding to the minor level of importance accorded local politics. An additional source of debilitation of local leadership results from the scattered suburban residence pattern that separates social and business status holders from the legal city and defines their civic competence and responsibility for them and others in an ambiguous way. The status of political leadership is frequently inadequate to mobilize support for more than the most routine forms of civic house-keeping. The capacity to deal with more important problems requires an exceptional effort to bring about a united front among major resource holders and a precarious local *union sacrée* of reluctant and marginal burghers. Even so seemingly powerful a figure as Richard Daley proceeds by implementing consensus. Banfield's account of Chicago while flattering to Daley's power evidences the consensual nature of the city's politics. Hunter's "Regional City" is the major example in the literature of a power-ful monolithic local leadership. Elsewhere the fragmentation of civic pluralism reigns. Even Hunter's all powerful elite are portrayed only in the rather trivial action of forming a world trade center.

Polsby's review of the community decision-making studies reveals the rather surprising inconsequentiality of the decisions made. While this might lead to a view that the local community has lost power to outside organizations and superior levels of government to such an extent as to trivialize its function, it is safer to assume that the triviality of the decisions is an artifact of the decisions studied and possibly of the decisional focus itself. If one reviews the handling of strikes from the thirties to the present in local communities, in many one finds that the prediction that the local police will be used to break strikes changes to one that the local police will be used to help strikers. This might be regarded as a community decision. However, it is extended in time and provides no dramatic focus on a set of specific decision makers. The response to a bus boycott in Montgomery is another type of decision that escapes the usual studies. School integration, housing, equal employment oppor-tunities, and other changes in access to the local opportunity structure are not trivial for those involved. These types of issues perhaps concern not so much decisions within a going system as much as changes in the system itself. Like much of the most fundamental political change they may involve incremental change in a pattern of habits that normally fails to surface. On occasion when the pace and intensity of this change creates major disparities between the habits of the *status quo* and new facts of expectations and power, overt political conflict and demand for decision making occur. For this kind of decision there may be no adequate political leadership or process.

Our government has been a limited one and our political institutions are designed for limited purposes. Except for the early days when New Englanders were seeking a New Jerusalem and Indian and other hazards made universal service and mobilization a necessity for survival, our political communities have been Lockean remedies for the inconveniences of the state of nature, gradually developing into municipal service corporations to remedy the inconveniences of urban life. Large-scale commitment has been limited to war which we only gradually learned to wage in a serious way with the experience of the Civil War. Even war was regarded as an unnatural interruption of the normal private life of citizens. Waging war is the one purpose for which we are socialized to effective all-out mobilization of our resources. It is for this reason that the "War on Poverty" gets its name and, perhaps, because of the odious comparison with our efforts in a real war that to many this seems a phony war if not a publicity ploy. However, this is unfair. As a people we are not equipped with the ideas, habits, and institutions to wage anything in an all-out fashion other than war. Roosevelt's attack on the depression failed because it could only mobilize a tiny fraction of the resources that readily produced full employment in World War II. Only a few communities with extraordinary leadership reacting to disaster have even begun to enlist their citizens and their resources for massive sustained action, and in these cases the disaster and its remedy have been natural and material, requiring no politics of social reform or income redistribution.

The problems of the present urban condition are physical and social. Alarmists and those seeking to arouse alarm as a means of civic mobilization have been painting the blackest picture of our sick cities. Mitchell Gordon's book bearing that title comes to mind. A contrary view of well nigh general improvement is expressed by Raymond Vernon who finds little reality and much myth in the literature. Indeed he ascribes much of the outcry to the inconvenience of articulate members of the middle class who are incommoded by their journey to work and sentimentally attached to the cultural institutions of the the central city as well as being motivated by concern for the central business district.

In one view the physical and social condition is dramatically worsening; in the other it is dramatically improving. There is evidence for both.

Americans like to delegate their choices to experts and feel coerced into action by a scientifically determined value neutral logic. Perhaps one should say their ideology permits and encourages the formulation of social choice as the seeming non-choice of expert decision making. Doing what the doctor orders seems only good sense. By extension all social ills are pathology for which there should be appropriate doctors. Much of the history of metropolitan reform has been taken up with "scientific surveys" whose civic, business, and foundation sponsors hoped would convince all "thinking" men of their merits. This mood was portrayed in its full humor by a Dayton newspaper in a cartoon of Professor John Bollens equipped with black bag and stethescope captioned, "Thank you for coming, Dr. Bollens." The National Municipal League and its allies have propagated the view that local government is a business that should be free of politics run in a nonpartisan manner in accordance with the one best way. This is the public-regarding ethos celebrated in Banfield and Wilson's *City Politics*. By denying the validity of partisanship it seeks to monopolize the control of policy for the wise and the good who as with the Federalists turn out happily to be the middle class. The latest in the long line of local government reform literature is a pamphlet of the Committee for Economic Development which brashly calls for the wholesale euthanasia of redundant local governments. For the management experts and their academic advisors the problem is simply creating big governments that will include big resources, attract big men, and do big things in a big way. If one could only enclose the physical and social problems in an adequate territorial jurisdiction with adequate resources and with a streamlined government, some Bob Moses or Gardiner would get with the necessary job.

The coexistence of physical and social problems and their inextricable intermingling encourages an engineering view. Smog, water pollution, sewage, waste, housing, blight, traffic, transport, all seem to some matters of straightforward engineering. Their solutions should be free from politics. Or should they? Or can they? All the physical problems compete with each other and

with social problems for scarce resources. Any assumption that
there is conflictless affluence is fatuous. Beyond the context for
scarce resources there is the difficulty of creating political structures for their employment in problem solution. Consensus of a
sort can be brought to bear on physical problems, especially
when they create acute levels of discomfort, as metropolitan
Toronto has shown. But that rare example of metropolitan success
painfully illustrates the limited nature of the consensus when the
social problems of redistribution are confronted. A political structure adequate to deal with smog, sewage, water, and transport
might be capable and compelled to deal with housing, education,
and jobs, in a word the politics of social democracy. Alternatively
such a structure might dilute the central city power of the poor
and the Negro and reduce their bargaining strength. The urban
condition gives rise to demands for a social politics that limited
government and an ideology of individualism are undesigned
and unempowered to provide. We can, indeed we have, produced
organizations that can move physical mountains. Limited government and individualism have been quite capable of transform-
ing nature. But their capacity to transform social structure is
contradicted by their ideological commitment.

This limitation is frequently seen as stemming from inadequate
fiscal resources and government structure. Galbraith points to
what he finds the anomalous discrepancy between an affluent
federal government with limited needs and an impoverished local
government where the action is. It is certainly true that local
government leaders complain bitterly of their lack of funds. It is
equally true that the federal tax structure is a more effective
engine for revenue production than that possessed by states or
cities. Yet state and local governments have been far more responsive to the needs that Galbraith has in mind than has the
federal government whose social expenditures have lagged behind. This argues that both our ideology of government and the
effective political pressures permit and produce greater state and
local action than federal. For the fiscal problem a combination
of the local sense of urgency with the capacity of the federal tax
collector seems to some a promising solution. Certainly anything
approaching the dollars Mayor Lindsay says are needed for New
York's blight will scarcely come from anywhere but Washington.
However, even the most sympathetic Senators find this hope-

lessly unrealistic. This leaves the uncomfortable question as to whether Mayor Lindsay was in gross exaggeration or, as seems more likely, federal expenditures are designed as gestures rather than fiscally adequate solutions. Thus far the federal government has used its financial powers as bait rather than funding adequate to achieve major objectives. Whether in the Poverty Program or other areas, the federal role has been one of initiator delegating downward the responsibility for follow-through and effective action.

Constitutional scruples and a commitment to the ideology of laissez-faire have made federal intervention, except in agriculture, piecemeal and seemingly with a bad conscience. We have lacked and still lack any well-considered political philosophy to provide direction and consistency to government action. Since we are scarcely a decade from the great debate as to whether the power to spend for the general welfare permitted a welfare state and whether the latter was not an un-American abomination, this is scarcely surprising. Our commitment to social democracy while proclaimed with outrage by conservatives is as yet unaccepted publicly as other than a growing congeries of exceptions to the general rule of limited government and laissez-faire. The proliferation of epicycles required by this Ptolemaic theory is badly in need of a Copernican revision. In any event, the federal and the local governments are finding piecemeal federal interventions, intended and unintended, increasingly haphazard and contradictory. The great functional autocracies of the federal government and their state and local counterparts show little evidence of being guided by any invisible hand to produce local harmony. Federal lack of coordination is compounded by metropolitan fragmentation that up to now has resulted in the expediential fragmentation of federal efforts in the service of shoring up the local *status quo* in accordance with the alliances of bureaucratic politics and survival interests. The recent conversion of the federal government to metropolitan planning may be a passing fad or the beginning of an evolving national system of local government.

What we badly need is a theory of what we are about. With the Employment Act of 1948 we crossed the bridge of some serious national commitment to mind the state of the economy. The congeries of programs of the Great Society recognize that much besides this needs to be done. Pockets of stubborn depression and self-perpetuating misery exist in rural areas and cities. Gross educational failure despite dramatic improvements threatens more menacingly in a high-skill and increasingly automated economy. All of these recent federal interventions are demonstrations designed perhaps to test their political appeal, often to prime the pump of local action, but in almost all cases totally inadequate to meet the needs to which they are directed.

The Eisenhower Goals for America might have been a serious start toward at least indicative national planning. They appear to have been taken seriously neither by Eisenhower nor his successors. The National Planning Association has done us the service to cost them out. What this showed is that even these goals, considered by some rather modest, are far from easily in our reach. Priorities and choices would need to be adopted. Taking the Eisenhower Goals seriously could lead to our getting some grip on the means-ends chains by which they might be brought about. We could escape emulating the Mao Tse-tung enthusiasm which equates political will with availability of economic means. This might help us to arrive at a fair recognition of the capabilities of local government and the tasks it might appropriately perform in meeting our national goals, supposing we have a political leadership that can give them articulation and gain consensus for them.

The political philosophy of Jefferson with its emphasis on the sovereign individual, its distrust of all government especially the federal, and its hatred of the city is hopelessly inappropriate for a complex, interdependent, urban nation. In practice it results in the escapism of suburbia sentimentally seen as the modern equivalent of the New England town. Even the individualism of a society of educated, middle-class professionals and experts has little to offer beyond a condescending *noblesse oblige* as a reason for intervening in affairs for which it has neither avowed responsibility nor recognized shared common fate. The economists ranging from Friedman to Galbraith have done duty as our political philosophers, perhaps because thinking about an economy is the nearest thing we can do to thinking about a society or polity—which we are not prepared to do. A market basket of public goods is the appropriate goal of a society of consumers. But however much we have extended the meaning and importance of consumership to spectator sports, spectator politics, and a life of TVing it, there are limits to what can be purchased. A democratic society must in a sense be self-produced; it cannot be bought ready made. Much of what is important in such a society cannot be produced with money alone though money is critically important. Even the availability of money depends on a mobilization of will and purpose that is scarcely likely without major involvement. Involvement requires a sense of participation in a community with powerfully shared common purposes and an appropriate role structure for their attainment. With the Civil War and two world wars, a great depression and the creation of a continental economy, we have created a nation. For an affluent middle class we have created the conditions of privacy and individuality. These personal liberties are precious to those who have lost them. They are not merely selfish, for in their way they do insure public values. However, individualism today no longer has the challenge of an underdeveloped country. The valued by-products of its ruggedness in a crowded urban world are less clear. The emptiness of purpose so common in today's youth bespeaks the inadequacy of America's role structure. The anguish that Goodman describes as growing up absurd is not that of material poverty alone but is more keenly felt by those unstructured by the drives of want.

The nation enlists our loyalty. It is the master institution of the modern world. We may have to discover and create the city and local government as needed instruments for the accomplishment of keenly felt national purposes. In our past the nation arose from a limited purpose institution to meet the marginal needs of states that were themselves the creatures of towns and sovereign individuals hardly out of the state of nature. A reverse process may now be underway. The growing federal emphasis on metropolitan planning and plan implementation is a step toward using the federal carrot and perhaps the federal stick toward creating a nationally relevant set of metropolitan governments. The proposal for a federal coordinator in the demonstration cities is another straw in the wind. The Great Society, though a casualty of the war in Vietnam, can scarely be more than postponed. While some of its confused debris of local agencies can be attributed to federal hesitation and qualms about direct intervention, a great deal of the effort to produce grass roots actively represents some real appreciation of the importance of local involvement for vitality and success. Even the ineffectual attempts at giving power and representation to the powerless poor are hopefully more than a passing fad. While much federal activity can be counted as mere downward buck-passing, some at least must be counted as representing genuine realization of the importance of an effective local government for the attainment of central government purposes. High among these purposes must be the restructuring of local government to reflect by the range of population and problems it is intended to deal with a need to respond to the order of concerns that are nationally salient.

A national politics that is increasingly social democratic in content requires a local government structure that is not at odds with it. This is not now the case. Our structure of local government in the metropolitan areas is designed as Wood says to segregate needs from resources. Even more it is designed to maintain our stratification system and this gives it powerful appeal. The charmed circle of our society runs from housing to education, to jobs and matrimony, to income, and back to housing if one is not discriminated against in its purchasing. While education was purchased in the private market, rationing by price avoided overt public discrimination. In the middle-class society, education has become a public good. Providing different qualities of education to formally equal citizens has been solved by suburbanized segregation of its consumption. The federal goals of redistributive politics have required opening access to the opportunity structure for the disadvantaged, particularly Negroes. This means in practice jobs, but access to jobs requires education and access to education requires access to housing. This has meant that major federal social goals can only be attained with the cooperation of local governments whose orientation is toward the maintenance of segregated public goods consumption. For this reason federal purposes of social reform are impelled to press for local government reform. These pressures are reinforced by the jurisdictional inadequacies of existing local governments to deal with smog, water pollution, traffic, and other matters of middle-class discontent. The reform of our physical environment becomes entangled with the reform of our social environment. Agreement on the one does not presuppose agreement on the other, but both in their way point to a common shared fate that may be escaped by individual flight or overcome by collective action.

The national concern with social problems and their implications for government action and structure is met by a thrust from the cities. Those of them large enough to evoke leaderships with imagination, responsibility, and professional competence are increasingly aware of the interrelation of their social and economic problems. They rapidly outgrow the narrow perspective of brick and mortar urban renewal and arrive at some conception of development planning that in principle concerns itself with the systematic management of all the community's assets. In this they resemble the leadership of new nations, though both in some ways freer and in others more circumscribed. Henry Mayer, the mayor of Milwaukee, in his *Challenge to the Cities* gives a good example of an emerging approach and philosophy. His attempt to build a vital local citizenship for his city by exercising leadership in its economic, educational, and cultural life is a fine example of the politics of community building. The Milwaukee idea that he propounds is the national, city, state concept of an exciting shared common fate, a Burkean compact that unites economy, culture, the whole life of the city in a sense of purpose and destiny that can give the lives of a number of the citizens, enough to leaven the civic lump, a heightened sense of meaning. By tying together business, education, culture, recreation, and all the key pursuits of leading elements of the city in a sense of interrelated contributions to the future of the city, Maier hopes to unite, inspire, and transform the existing civic leaderships making them more fully accept a conscious, salient role as citizens. Maier, like the builders of the new nations, is in the business of making Milwaukee citizens. He is teaching them new roles so that hopefully they may find significant and challenging ways to enhance the merely private life of individualism and consumership.

Milwaukee nationalism has its points like the classical, mediaeval, and the renaissance city; the modern city may be able to offer its local citizens a set of vigorous appealing roles that are not available to them in the macrosphere of the nation. Perhaps a better-designed federalism may even make national, state, and local roles effectively available in a context of local action where geared to common purposes they mesh in programmatic cooperation.

Our traditional political technology is based on the symbolism of territorial government. The socialized culture inculcates attitudes toward hallowed ground, the graves of our ancestors, shared history. These symbols make possible the category of fellow townsmen for whom it is fitting and right for us to care in a quite different fashion from the external "they" that are outside the fellow citizen "we." At the level of state and local government, and in some ways especially the latter, a general policy power for a multitude of public objects escaped the doctrinal damnation of laissez-faire. As Beard points out we were after a fashion municipal socialists when Herbert Spencer's Social Darwinism rode high in the nation. The cities on a hill, the New Jerusalems of Puritan imagining, even the New Harmonies have been essentially local. We have therefore a tradition of potential shared meanings in our local communities upon which one might hope to build communities of common purpose that might bridge the gaps between classes, races, and other divisions in an overarching conception of a mutually meaningful civic enterprise. However good our intentions in Washington, the reality of the quality of the national purpose is where most people must embody it in their daily lives. The paratroopers in Little Rock and the marshals in Mississippi may be necessary to make the federal writ run, but only local leaderships can ultimately produce the transformation in local behavior. Local examples of a unified community planning, supporting, producing within the range of their powers an exciting challenging common fate have far greater power than federal compulsion. The power of a real example, of the spate of slogans and preaching given the visible sincerity of concrete action, has the force of the propaganda of the deed, the only ultimately successful means of persuasion.

Mayor Maier's conception of a city planning and producing its social, economic, and cultural life has a powerful appeal to an unsatisfied need of human beings for the warmth and significance of shared community, for a structure to provide a worthy set of purposes and roles, and a theatre of action in which audience and cast interchange roles and create the script that expresses their pursuit of their city on a hill. This is certainly a way, perhaps the only way, that there is hope of socializing local citizens with commitment to running the local railroad, a commitment that derives from a shared commitment to its importance and general direction. Worthy as Mayor Maier's Milwaukee idea is it is amazingly weak in the conception of its implementation. The script reads the hero mayor arousing fitfully a reluctant and lethargic populace, with difficulty communicating through a malign media, sharing himself with a corporals' guard of grudgingly provided professionals, achieving precarious and evanescent combinations of notables to engineer community decisions, and at best achieving some change in city or environing institutions that will outlive his brief tenure and waning personal influence. In his appreciation of means to very substantial ends, Mayor Maier is almost as anemic as the National Municipal League if not as legalistic and naively managerial as the Committee for Economic Development. The mayor shares a belief in a combination of individual executive leadership with a professional bureaucracy to instrument it with a diplomacy of notable involvement that is common to federal bureaucrats and many academics. The powers in our society are the large bureaucratic organizations, school systems, police departments, public utilities, and corporations. These are the institutions that mobilize resources, have a long-term sustained thrust and move mountains. Their logic and the market, unintended, logic of their interplay produce the main outlines of the future. Against these massive unplanned forces, the mayor and his corporals' guard of professionals pit their wits hoping with minor resources of exhortation and funds to find the social fulcra on which they too with pygmy strength may move their mountains. One should not underestimate the mayor's power as preacher and educator. The ritual priesthood of the norms is a major, if not *the* major, function of political leadership. But this is by and large a conservative function. What Mayer is hoping to do is out of traditional elements to rewrite the script and produce a changed definition of the situation. This requires an appropriate politics.

A politics that hopes to plan and coordinate the massive bureaucratic institutions of our society in the service of a broadly conceived program of community ends must solve the problem of power. This problem is measured by the power of the program to achieve the mobilization and enlistment of adequate human and material resources. Without minimizing the importance of material resources, the human component is not only essential to sustained material mobilization it is essential to the alteration of massive behaviors that cannot merely be purchased. The alteration of slum behavior, lower-class behavior, suburban middle- and lower-middle-class behavior is not simply a matter of professional skill plus a treasury. It cannot be reduced to the antiseptic professionalism of the managers either C.E.D. or old style I.C.M. What is required, if more than expensive and noble gestures are intended, is a serious, intense, and in-depth politics.

The politics of community development which is what the Milwaukee idea is all about requires, if it is to have adequate power and sustained drive, a political vehicle that makes the means commensurate with the ends in view. Since what is envisioned is similar in kind if different in degree to what the developing nations are concerned with, in the one case making a nation and creating national citizens and in the other creating a community and community citizens, it may be helpful to look at their key political instrumentality. This is a broad, ideological party of community mobilization that in principle can effectively empower a leadership for sustained programmatic action. City builders need to consider whether their serious ends can be seriously undertaken with any less potent instrument for popular involvement and support. In the past, the intellectuals of local government have sometimes called for local parties. Where they have done so it has usually been for highly limited purposes of middle-class honest government reform. In almost all cases it has been designed to make local parties less rather than more programmatic by severing them from the partisan politics of state and national parties. These latter in all conscience as almost strictly electoral parties are programmatically anemic themselves. As Edward Banfield has pointed out we are increasing the burden of local government by giving it major tasks at a time when civil service reform and "good government" have drastically reduced the available rewards at the disposal of local political leaderships. The old machine at least had the merit of reaching down through its ward organization to the people. It had cadres of a sort to achieve some kind of effective popular mobilization. The media politicians of the newspaper wards are without vital human connection with the people where they live. Their power is fragile, liable to reverses from blind and ill-appreciated resentments vented in voting booths at bond or charter elections. The power expresses itself most effectively as a conspiracy of notables engineered by city hall to achieve concerted institutional support for civic projects.

This power is most ineffectual to bring about major social change whether the social change is restructuring slum behaviors or restructuring white behavior to permit open occupancy and integrated education. Delusions have been spread by the social science fiction of C. Wright Mills and Floyd Hunter who take the conspiracy of notables with the hero mayor as puppet as a kind of minor league executive committee of the bourgeoisie. This piece of vulgar Marxism sees the problem of power as solved ready made through an automatically produced hierarchy of business and wealth. Where Marx saw capitalism as a system of great power with well-rewarded but powerless capitalists functioning as driven cogs in an unplanned and hence doomed order, these latter-day revisionists have created the myth of the power structure. Civil rights leaders who have attended this school seek vainly to force a confrontation with a white power structure who could if it only would grant their demands. Nothing is more touching than Martin Luther King calling off his marches for a summit conference with a Chicago white power structure composed of Daley and a parcel of businessmen and clerics who accord him open occupancy for his people. This is the C.E.D. drama of the big men in a big city doing big things without benefit of politics. The fatuousness of this "power structure" pretending to massively change the behavior of the white ethnics of Cicero or elsewhere must have been clear even to the participants at the time. That none of them seriously intended to organize themselves and others for the long-term struggle to alter behavior massively seems equally clear. What was involved was at best a piece of civic ritual and at worst a publicity ploy. This kind of white magic is a delusion common to the power structure enthusiasts and the managerialists of local government reform, C.E.D. or other.

It is seriously interesting to ask what kind of politics is relevant to meeting Martin Luther King's demand for open occupancy or the legal or hopefully more than legal compliance with civil rights legislation. For ends of this magnitude and difficulty we really need to wage a war. But the waging of war requires more than the low budget spectacular of a Poverty Program with its bag of good intentions and its harvest of publicity. It is something far more significant and difficult than stodging together new bureaucratic enterprise and giving it a petty cash account and hunting license to win enough public favor to stay in business. What is required is an ideological party with a mass base dedicated to the pursuit of the objectives Mayor Mayer finds challenging our cities. These challenges are no small affair. They amount to a social and economic program of mobilizing the total resources of the community behind a planned effort to achieve its overall development. Taken seriously this amounts to an American variant of social democracy at the local level. It would require the full range of energies that James Wilson has described in the club movement and would need to penetrate far below this thin layer of middle-class amateurs. The cadres of a party dedicated to tough long-term goals need more than the motivation of a lonely hearts club. This means perhaps seeming as fanatical as Goldwaterites or Birchers though hopefully with more humane, relevant, and feasible objectives. A party that is concerned with planning and running a city in accordance with a powerful set of convictions could recruit the personnel to structure and man a sustained attack on the problems of the city seen as both challenge and opportunity to shape the human condition.

The failure of merely managerial efforts at urban reform has largely stemmed from blindness to face or unwillingness or inability of a politics of sustained, broad-based action. The politics of metropolitan reform has been a politics of foundation surveys, laying on of the hands of business and civic notables, and ineffective media campaigns. The question of who really seriously wants to do anything in a sustained way has never been met. If the goals for our cities are revolutionary we need to face the need for a revolution in our politics to attain them. Such a revolution can only be made by a party committed to them not by a managerial *coup d'état*. We can be administered from above. We can be self-governed only from below. A creative politics to bring about a committed urban citizenship requires a party with an ideology committed to its attainment. Such a party is the means for providing a program of action that can make citizenship at the local level a significant vocation. With such a party the cause of creating self-governing metropolitan areas capable of major social, economic, and cultural undertakings ceases to be the plaything of civic do-gooders and becomes an issue of deadly serious politics.

SELECTED REFERENCES

Banfield, Edward C., *Political Influence* (New York: The Free Press, 1961).

Boorstin, Daniel J., *The Lost World of Thomas Jefferson* (Boston: Beacon Press, 1960).

Dahl, Robert A., *Who Governs? Democracy and Power in an American City* (New Haven: Yale University Press, 1961).

Galbraith, John Kenneth, *The Affluent Society* (Boston: Houghton Mifflin Company, 1958).

Hunter, Floyd, *The Community Power Structure* (Chapel Hill: University of North Carolina Press, 1953).

Maier, Henry, *Challenge to the Cities* (New York: Random House, 1966).

Polsby, Nelson, *Community Power and Political Theory* (New Haven: Yale University Press, 1963).

Wilson, James Q., *Club Politics in Three Cities* (Chicago: University of Chicago Press, 1962).

**III  Some Larger Contexts of Community Institutions**

# 8 Urban Goals and Economic Growth

## Lyle C. Fitch

The approach of this paper was inspired by one of the first modern treatises on political economy—Sir William Petty's *Political Arithmetick* (published in 1690), which he begins by saying: ". . . I have taken the course . . . to express myself in Terms of *Number, Weight,* or *Measure;* to use only Arguments of Sense, and to consider only such Causes, as have visible Foundations in Nature." Like Petty, I have stuck to numbers and measures, and, I hope, used only arguments of sense.

But my subject emphasizes how far we are removed from Petty in other respects. Those concerned with political economy and the art of government, for nearly two and a half centuries after the publication of Petty's book, paid small attention to either urban goals or economic growth. True, Adam Smith's great treatise was entitled *An Enquiry into the Nature and Causes of the Wealth of Nations,* but Smith was engaged chiefly in demonstrating that economies would grow most rapidly if governments kept hands off economic affairs, *i.e.,* if there were no attempts to pursue central goals. His interest in cities was in their role as centers of trade and manufacturing, which in turn promoted specialization of labor—the key to economic development. This conviction was echoed and reinforced by the generations of classical political economists who followed him.

Smith began with an observation that has great pertinence today, however, in saying that the nation's supply of "necessaries and conveniences" must be "regulated by two different circumstances; first, the skill, dexterity, and judgment with which its

labour is generally applied; and secondly by the proportion between the number of those who are employed in useful labour,
and that of those who are not so employed." [1] Today we refer to
the first "circumstance" as "productivity of labor," and to the
second as "rate of participation in the labor force."

In the heyday of the classical political economists, which was
the middle half of the nineteenth century, Smith's first observation about the importance of skill and dexterity was more or less
forgotten. Labor came to be regarded as a necessary but low-
grade commodity, like something to be purchased from a foreign
country as cheaply as possible. This led to the convenient notion
that the laboring population as a class could rise only by limiting
its numbers and that public policies to improve the lot of labor
could only make matters worse. The first notion still has partial
validity; the latter notion is fairly dead, though its tail is still
wiggling. Now we think of labor as a resource to be developed
through investments in health, general education, and specific
training; this concept gained general acceptance only after the
Second World War.

Concern for the lot of the poor and downtrodden and with
the wretched condition of the early industrial cities was not
lacking in the nineteenth century, but the reformers of the time
were not prone to regard economic growth and greater productivity as a solution; rather, they sought a redistribution of wealth,
an end to private ownership of the means of production, and a
drastically changed social order where everyone would be on a
more equal footing.

We have learned since that modern production requires large
organizations, which look and operate about the same whether
they are under private or public management. Government
ownership of the means of production is not the magic solution,
and for good and sufficient reasons may be an inferior solution
in many cultures today. Nor is merely dividing the pie more
equally a solution; the effect is usually to share the poverty rather
than the wealth. But economic growth, which received relatively
little attention in the nineteenth and early twentieth centuries
as an instrument of social reform, has greatly simplified the
problems of reform—instead of fighting about the division of the
pie, make the pie bigger and let everybody have more. So it is

that the dire forebodings of the Malthusians and the Marxists have thus far been disproven, or at least fended off, by the astonishing growth of productivity in the technological age.

This exercise in political arithmetic begins with the question: will the United States in the foreseeable years have enough resources to meet its urban goals? Put that way, the question is like asking if a ladder is long enough to reach a ceiling without specifying either the length of the ladder or the height of the ceiling. Nonetheless, the prophets of the affluent society have been assuring us that we are now so very productive that we can have virtually anything we want if we will only make up our minds as to what we want and go after it. But down at the level of urban governments, where the urban problems are, things look much less simple—city governments everywhere are desperately short of money. It seems, as Wilfred Owen has pointed out in another context, that even if nationally we are very rich, locally we are very poor.

When I speak of resources, I refer specifically to the gross national product, which is the value of all the goods and services produced for the market.[2] The GNP is a pretty good index, but by no means a complete measure, of how well off we are. It omits, for example, the value of all services that are not directly paid for, including the services of housewives in their many capacities. It also omits the do-it-yourself crowd—if you build your own boat or paint your house, the value of the work you do is not counted whereas it would be if you hired someone to do the same work. It fails to take account of the subtractions from well-being like air and water pollution emitted in the course of production. Most urban goals, however, require inputs which get counted in the GNP, and it is therefore not a bad measure to use in assessing capacity to achieve urban goals.

The gross national product and its components are analogous to sales, cost, and profits figures for a private firm and are watched by those concerned with national economic performance as carefully as are profit and loss statements of a private firm by its management and stockholders (not to mention the Director of Internal Revenue). Much of the country's economic policy is devoted to making the GNP go up, while keeping prices stable. J. K. Galbraith recently observed that for the last two decades St. Peter's first question to any candidate at the Pearly Gates has been, "What have you done to increase the gross national product?"

Having crossed the river Jordan into the Keynesian promised land of continued high levels of prosperity and continuously increasing GNP, we are now becoming more interested in the uses to which the GNP should be put, that is to say, with formulating various kinds of goals, and with projecting the costs of goals. The Eisenhower Commission on National Goals set the fashion; more recently many communities and metropolitan areas have gone to work to formulate goals for their own development (Dallas, Los Angeles, Phoenix, to name a few). So formulating goals and making projections—that is, planning—are increasingly popular indoor sports nowadays. While projection-making has a following which is only minor league compared to that of its ancient rival, astrology, at least projections are becoming respectable, and planning is no longer regarded as *ipso facto* subversive. The most substantial effort at the long-run guessing game on the national scale is that of the National Planning Association, which recently published *Goals, Priorities, & Dollars* (by Leonard A. Lecht), being an attempt to set several goals into the framework of the gross national product demand schedule, and to see if the supply of gross national product could meet the demand in Year X (in this case 1975). Lecht specifies quantitative goals in sixteen different areas including consumption, urban development, health, welfare, and education, transportation and housing.[3] He then asks: What would be the cost in 1975 of meeting these goals? It turns out that the gross national product at *its* projected growth rate falls short of the demands posed by the aspiration goals. This is because Lecht assumes that the gross national product (on the supply side) will grow at a rate of 4 percent, while the components of the demand side, to be quantitatively consistent with goals, will grow at rates exceeding 4 percent. The demand therefore outruns the supply in the target year.

The present exercise in political arithmetic asks a somewhat different question, to wit: What is the total amount of resources with which we shall have to work from now until the end of the century? It then proceeds to examine some of the things which might be done within the total. The aggregate product which may accrue between now and the end of the century is a somewhat better gauge of our capacity for achievement than the gross national product for a single year. For a single year, the demand side may be heavily weighted by attempts to catch up with accumulated deficiencies, or to make investments which will pay out only gradually.

I next set down some specific goals,[4] as a means for focusing thinking. In the broad, there are two main categories:

1. Eradicating poverty and discrimination, and
2. Improving the urban environment as to efficiency and aesthetic quality.

Within these categories we can specify some more detailed goals, including:

1. Lifelong educational opportunities, designed to give each person full opportunity to develop his own capacities.
2. Health and medical services adequate to allow each person to achieve his full potential productivity and sense of physical well-being.
3. Decent and adequate housing.
4. A variety of cultural and recreational opportunities.
5. Job opportunities for all who wish to work.
6. Assured incomes for those unable to work, sufficient for a decent standard of living.
7. Freedom from personal and environmental aggression (as from obtrusive noise, polluted air, overcrowding).
8. A variety of ways of life and opportunities to choose among them, such as a greater degree of choice among all income groups between living in central cities or suburbs without unduly sacrificing essential amenities (such as educational opportunities, physical safety, fresh air, or mobility).
9. Central cities maintained as vital, healthy centers of business, knowledge, and culture, management, commercial activity, and residences.
10. Planned metropolitan development outside central cities with population and activities grouped into urban sub-centers designed for efficiency and aesthetic appeal.

Of the factors which bear upon the nation's ability to meet goals in the last third of the century, three stand out as overwhelmingly important. First is the size of the Year-2000 population. Second is the growth rate of the gross national product. Third is the proportion of GNP that goes for private consumption, simply because this is the major use of GNP and far overshadows other demand components.

## SIZE OF POPULATION

We enter the last third of the twentieth century with a population close to 200,000,000.[5] When we were still projecting the population increase rates of the 1950s, it looked as though the U.S. population by the Year-2000 might be over 400,000,000. This implied that the country's urban population would more than double in the last third of the century. But the birth rate has been falling rather sharply in the 1960s as more and more people "take to the pills," and the demographers have been revising population projections downward in consequence. The Bureau of the Census high population for the Year-2000 is about 360,000,000; the low projection, which now appears to be the best bet of its four projections, is about 280,000,000. So let's say that the Year-2000 population will range between 280,000,000 and 360,000,000, representing an increase of 40–80 percent over the present level.

There are several notable things about the Year-2000 population. First is that fact that the proportion of people in the working-age bracket (20–64 years) will increase much more than the population at large. This age bracket comprises about 46 percent of the present population, but in the Year-2000 it would be about 56 percent of the low projection (280,000,000) and 52 percent of the high projection (360,000,000). Second, the working-age group of the Year-2000 would not vary greatly as between the two population projections—it will not be heavily affected by what happens to the birth rate from here on because something like two thirds of it has already been born. The high population projection is about 29 percent over the low projection, but the corresponding working-age group high projection is only 20 percent over the low projection.

The 80,000,000 population differential between the Year-2000 high and low projections, of course, consists of people who would be born (if they were born) between now and the end of the century. A high proportion of the differential would be under twenty, and a high proportion would be in school. In fact, the in-school population, in accordance with the education goals I am projecting, would be about half of the total differential population.

The 80,000,000 differential thus would require high expenditures on education in addition to costs of housing, infrastructure, and ordinary maintenance. The marginal contribution of the differential working force at best would fall considerably short of supporting the differential population because the working force proportion is so low.

What of the implications for the gross national product of the population differential? I have already noted that the marginal product turned out by the differential population would not be sufficient to support the differential population—this means that the smaller population would enjoy a higher product-per-person than the larger. In fact, there are some reasons for supposing that the total gross national product for a population even as large as 360,000,000 would be little if any larger than that for a 280,000,000 population.

First, because the incremental population would not be self-supporting, the pool of funds for savings and capital formation would be larger for the smaller population.

Second, a relatively high proportion of the differential population would come from the low-income, low-culture groups. They will require relatively high investments in education and acculturation to get them out of the poverty trap in any case, and the productivity of those going into the labor force is bound to be relatively low, no matter what we can do in the meantime.

Third, the continued march of technology may continue to deplete jobs for low- and semiskilled workers, and make part of the differential labor force redundant. Present indications are that the problems of unemployment in the nonwhite city ghettos will increase, at least in the next several years.

GROSS NATIONAL PRODUCT PROJECTIONS

This gets us to the projected magnitude of the gross national product itself. The commonest prescription for projections is as follows:

1. Project the labor force in terms of manhours available. This magnitude is in part a function of population projection and in part of economic and cultural preferences for paid work as against leisure (or nonpaid work).

2. Project trends in productivity for workers, which leads directly to output per worker.
3. Multiply output per worker by the number of workers.

I have suggested that this formula may not apply so well to the rest of this century because of the probable composition of the population differential (as between low and high projections), because the differential labor force might be of low productivity or even redundant, and because capital formation per worker might be lower for a larger population. So I shall depend more on extrapolation for my projection.

What rate of increase in real GNP (value of goods and services at 1966 prices) can we reasonably project? GNP growth rate between 1929 and 1960 was about 3 percent, but growth was interrupted by nearly a decade while the nation went through the agony of the great depression. The rate between 1947 and 1966 was nearly 4 percent. Between 1952 and 1960, a period often cited by the Democrats for obvious reasons, the rate was about 2.6 percent, but between 1960 and 1966 it was in the magnitude of 4.9 percent.

Now here is the important part. A 3 percent growth rate for the rest of the century will give us an aggregate gross national product of about $42.5 trillion. A 4 percent rate, which nowadays is commonly thought to be reasonable, would give us $51.5 trillion. *The difference, $9 trillion, is equal to about thirteen years gross national product at present levels.* A 4½ percent growth rate, which is not entirely out of the question, would provide an aggregate GNP of some $56.5 trillion.

Thus, the most important requirement for achieving our urban goals is to keep up the rate of economic growth. This will require high rates of investment in productive facilities (plant equipment, research and development) and in education. Education of the low-productivity groups is an important factor. The Council of Economic Advisers 1965 Report estimated that if the nonwhite population were brought up to the equivalent of the white in education and earnings, the gross national product in 1965 would have been $27 billion higher. Over the rest of the century, this differential would cumulate to some $1.5 trillion.

Edward Denison's study for the Committee for Economic Development, *The Sources of Economic Growth in the United*

*States and the Alternatives Before Us,* attributes 23 percent of GNP increases between 1929 and 1957 to advances in education, 20 percent to advances of knowledge, but only 15 percent to increases in the stock of capital per se. (Denison's own projections, incidentally, indicate a 3.33 percent annual increase in real national income over the period 1960–1980.)

CONSUMPTION

Consumption—by which we mean personal expenditures on consumer goods—is the key to several high-priority goals.

First is the fact that consumption of the poor and the near-poor, who constitute a fourth of the present population, is woefully deficient and should be raised forthwith.

Second, the category of consumer expenditures covers a substantial part of several other important goals including improved health, housing, transportation, and education.

Third, the greater the proportion of GNP spent for consumption, the less there is left for public services and investment-type expenditures on physical and social capital.

Fourth, if consumption lags behind increases in productive capacity, the GNP growth rate is likely to slow down unless the public sector moves to keep demand high.[6]

The most straightforward way of eradicating poverty is to provide the poor with more consumption power, first by income-increasing measures, and second by various services, such as low-cost housing, medical services, and so on.

There are two routes to increasing income. For those able to work, and whom we would ordinarily expect to see working, the solution is to increase skills and productivity and job opportunities. This group constitutes about 45 percent of those now classified as poor. For the others—the old, the sick and disabled, the mothers of fatherless families—the solution is to increase income allotted under various income maintenance programs—including social security and public assistance. (For the most part, the so-called income-maintenance plans are really income transfers, whereunder A is taxed to provide more income for B. This kind of transaction does not directly affect the gross national product; it only changes the identity of the purchasers thereof.)

Let us first explore the possibility of approximately doubling per capita consumption under a formula which by the Year-2000 would increase the consumption of the bottom quintile of consumers (the very poorest) by an average of 150 percent, the top quintile by 50 percent and the in-between quintiles by in-between percentages. This goal would raise the consumption of the average household in the bottom quintile to approximately $7,000, from the present figure of approximately $2,800. Consumption in the top bracket, by contrast, would go from $15,200 to $22,800.

But even by increasing the consumption of the poor by a factor of two and one-half is a slow train for the very poor, if we spread out this increase between now and Year-2000. The average annual increase in consumption per family, in the lowest quintile, would be only $125. Consider an alternative, more generous, formula, under which the per capita consumption of the lowest quintile would increase by 250 percent (that is, by a factor of 3.5) and that of the highest quintile by 50 percent, again with the in-between quintiles getting in-between amounts. Reaching this goal by the Year-2000 would serve to increase the average per family consumption of the poorest quintile by an annual amount of $210. The following table sums up the effects of the two proposed formulae.

## FORMULA 1

| Per Capita Increase by Quintiles | | Aggregate Consumption Between 1967 and 2000 Assuming 2000 Population Grows to | |
|---|---|---|---|
| Quintile | Percent of Increase | 280 million | 360 million |
| Bottom | 150 | | |
| Second | 125 | | |
| Third | 100 | | |
| Fourth | 75 | | |
| Top | 50 | $26.3 trillion | $29.2 trillion |

## FORMULA 2

| | | | |
|---|---|---|---|
| Bottom | 250 | | |
| Second | 200 | | |
| Third | 150 | | |
| Fourth | 100 | | |
| Top | 50 | $31.0 trillion | $32.5 trillion |

Consumption is now running at about 64 percent of GNP. If we assume that GNP grows at 3 percent, then aggregate GNP between 1967 and 2000 will be $42.6 trillion, so that only the lowest of the four estimates of aggregate consumption would be less than 64 percent of aggregate GNP. It would not be possible to use the more generous Formula 2 without increasing the share of consumption in GNP. If we assume instead a 4 percent growth rate of GNP (with an aggregate GNP between 1967 and 2000 of $51.6 trillion), then all four of the above estimates of aggregate consumption are less than 64 percent of aggregate GNP. Even were the population to grow at the highest rate projected for it, the generous Formula 2 could be used to increase per capita consumption without increasing the proportionate demand on GNP by more than the present level of 64 percent.

The goal of increases for everybody, with proportionately larger consumption increases for lower-income groups, would result in narrowing relatively the consumption differentials. In absolute dollars, however, they would be somewhat widened as between quintile averages (hopefully this effect would mollify at least some of the opposition to any income-consumption redistribution measures). However, any measures for narrowing the income and consumption differentials, whether by increasing productivity and earnings of those at the bottom or by income transfers, will almost certainly continue to encounter hot opposition.

Various other social welfare measures which might in fact narrow income and consumption differentials, such as education and health services, and other services provided directly by governments, show up in government purchases rather than in personal consumption purchases and are not taken into account here.

*Housing.* In formulating a goal for Year-2000 housing, I have set the following standards:

1. A dwelling unit for each of the 40,000,000 or more households which will be added in the interim.
2. Second dwelling units for 25 percent of the population.
3. Replacement to sufficiently bring the average age of the housing stock down to twenty-five years—which would require 47.5 million units.[7]

I have also assumed that the real cost of dwelling units would gradually increase from the 1967 average of $14,000 to a Year-2000 figure of approximately $22,500, with the proviso that the cost of second houses will average $10,000 less than other dwelling units. The total cost of housing, thus computed, is in the magnitude of $1.53 trillion for the low projection of population, and $1.94 trillion for the high projection.

*Education.* Here several factors need improvement. The average amount spent per child in elementary school and high school, in 1966, was in the magnitude of $600 per pupil, and if we may assume that the amount per secondary school student averages twice that of elementary school students, the amounts were $470 per elementary school pupil and $940 per secondary school pupil. Expenditures per college student, for those in undergraduate and postgraduate work, average $2,700 per student. I assume that we can look for eventual enrollment rates on the order of 99 percent of the age 5–13 age group, 95 percent of the 14–17 age group, 50 percent of the 18–21 group, 25 percent of the 22–24 group, and 10 percent of the 25–34 group. Assuming that these enrollment rates are reached by 1975, we get the following figures for the demand for schooling in terms of pupil years from 1967 to the year 2000.

| School Level | Aggregate Pupil Years, 1967–2000 | |
| | High Projection [a] | Low Projection [a] |
| --- | --- | --- |
| Elementary | 1.67 billion | 1.3  billion |
| Secondary | .63 billion | .53 billion |
| College and University | .54 billion | .47 billion |

[a] High projection is based on projection of 360,000,000 for Year-2000. Low projection is based on the projection of 280,000,000.

Costs of education will undoubtedly rise. With the need to pour enormously more funds into the education of low-income, low-culture groups, the advent of new and costly teaching technologies, and the continuing need for improvement of education overall, I think that a goal which contemplates doubling the average expenditure by 1975 is not unreasonable. If we assume costs to increase to this level by 1975, we get a grand figure for the cost of education between 1967 and 2000 of $5.3 trillion (for a high projection of Year-2000 population) and $4.4 trillion (for a low projection).

INFRASTRUCTURE

Infrastructure is the sixty-four-dollar word we use to describe the public capital needed to support the community—the transportation facilities, water and sewer lines, recreational and cultural facilities, public health centers and hospitals, etc. The estimated costs of furnishing infrastructure vary a good deal— the Regional Plan Association's estimates of costs in the New York region for new growth were in the magnitude of $18,000 per new household, and for replacement and modernization $2,200 each for all households as of the target date (1985). More recent estimates compiled for the Joint Committee on Economic Report, for the period 1966–1975, indicate a new-growth magnitude of about $20,000 per new household and a figure for modernization of $1,400 per household (as of 1975).

In my judgment these figures are a bit on the modest side; I would raise them a bit for the 1967–1975 period. For the period 1975–2000 I have used a cost figure of $30,000 for new infrastructure per new household and $5,000 per household (as of the Year-2000) for modernization and renewal.

These increases allow a fair margin for such things as improved pollution control, development and introduction of new transportation devices (separation of vehicular and pedestrian traffic, moving sidewalks, new mass transportation technologies). The total comes to a figure between $2 and $1.5 trillion; the magnitude might be increased by another 50 percent without profoundly changing the aggregate demand on GNP.

DOMESTIC PRIVATE BUSINESS INVESTMENT IN PLANT
AND EQUIPMENT

This category represents an amalgam of increasing capital plant and equipment and technological improvement. To the extent that research and development expenditures are capitalized, they are included in this figure; otherwise, they are included with consumption. It is the most difficult figure to project, because we have very little to go on to the functional relationship between private gross business investment and gross national product. As previously noted, Denison attributes 15 percent of the gross national product growth rate between 1929 and 1957 to the growth in stock of capital and another 20 percent to technological improvements. Throughout the postwar period, investment in P and E has stayed close to 10 percent, the average in the ten-year period 1956–66 is almost exactly 10 percent. During the high-growth period of the 1960s, the average has been a bit lower.

A substantial proportion of this outlay, however, represented investments in the space and defense industries. Meanwhile, it appears that many American industries are obsolescing technologically, so that in a number of fields U.S. industry is falling behind foreign competitors.[8]

Obsolescence is speeded up, moreover, by the pace of accelerating technology and the probability of demand for new types of consumer goods. The very large investment required to produce a supersonic transport is a straw in the wind. Increased emphasis on labor-saving devices, to accommodate the demands for more leisure, is still another element.

Still another type of demand that will raise the cost of plant and equipment is emerging in the form of new urban development technologies, ranging from pollution-control devices and new types of transportation vehicles to new technologies for housing and other construction, and requirements for greater aesthetic quality. The day is passing when smelly, ugly factories will be tolerated simply because they provide jobs.

Finally, there is the problem of maintaining a high rate of growth over an extended period of time—this may require substantially larger capital inputs than we have been accustomed to in the past.

I have shown two figures for investment in plant and equipment—one an aggregate figure of 10 percent of the gross national product, which is close to the historical average, and the other a figure of 15 percent. The 10 percent figure would take $5.1 trillion and the 15 percent figure $7.7 trillion, if we assume a 4 percent GNP growth rate, and $4.3 trillion and $6.4 trillion (respectively) if we assume a 3 percent GNP growth rate.

FEDERAL GOVERNMENT PURCHASES

Here the problem centers on what will happen to military expenditures. These are by far the largest drain on the gross national product. (Federal expenditures for nonmilitary goods and services in 1966 were only $17 billion compared with $60 billion for military expenditures.) The bulk of the federal government's other expenditures are transfer expenditures, mostly for grants-in-aid, income maintenance, and interest payments on the debt. Moreover, the federal government's goods-and-services purchases have not been rising rapidly, in contrast to the zooming rise of federal transfer expenditures.[9]

There is nothing on the horizon, save possibly a vast acceleration in the space exploration program, that seems likely to change this picture. I am therefore projecting that federal nondefense purchases will remain at the present percentage (2.3) of the gross national product.

Defense expenditures can be viewed optimistically or pessimistically. I include two projections: first, that defense expenditures will average $50 billion a year for the rest of the century; second, that they will average $100 billion a year. This makes a difference of $2.1 trillion in federal expenditures over the period (equal, incidentally, to almost three years of GNP at present rates).

## STATE AND LOCAL GOVERNMENT PURCHASES

State and local government purchases in recent years have been the most rapidly increasing segment of GNP. Two major components, however, have already been projected under other headings—they are infrastructure costs and education. The remainder is largely personal services, such as those of law-enforcement officers, firemen, inspectors, sanitation men, health and medical services, etc., along with the administrators of the various welfare (consumption-increasing) functions. In the 1960s, the rate of most rapid recent growth, such service expenditures have been increasing at the rate of about 4.7 percent per year. Projecting this rate for the rest of the century gives an aggregate GNP of $2.1 trillion.

## OTHER EXPENDITURES

The other components of the gross national product are the foreign balance and inventory accumulation, both of which, for any given year, might be either positive or negative. Inventory does not accumulate over the years as do other components of GNP—it is sold off and shows up in other GNP components. Therefore its total in this picture would be at the most in the magnitude of $20 billion or so, meaning that the inventory change

TABLE 1

Projected Aggregate Demands on Gross National Product: 1967–2000

| | Year-2000 Population of 280,000,000 Projections * | | Year-2000 Population of 360,000,000 Projections * | |
| --- | --- | --- | --- | --- |
| | High | Low | High | Low |
| | (trillions) | | (trillions) | |
| Consumption | $31.0 | $26.3 | $32.5 | $29.2 |
| Housing | 1.6 | 1.6 | 1.9 | 1.9 |
| Education, total | 4.4 | 4.4 | 5.3 | 5.3 |
| Urban public facilities (infrastructure) | 1.5 | 1.5 | 2.0 | 2.0 |
| Business investment (plant and equipment) | 7.7 | 4.3 | 7.7 | 4.3 |
| Federal government | | | | |
| Defense | 4.2 | 2.1 | 4.2 | 2.1 |
| Other | 1.2 | 1.0 | 1.2 | 1.0 |
| State and local government (excluding education and public facilities) | 1.8 | 1.8 | 1.8 | 1.8 |
| Foreign balance | 1.0 | .8 | 1.0 | .8 |
| TOTALS | $54.4 | $43.8 | $57.6 | $48.4 |

Aggregate GNP with Annual Growth of $\begin{cases} 4 \text{ percent} = \$51.5 \text{ trillion} \\ 3 \text{ percent} = \$42.5 \text{ trillion} \end{cases}$

* Principal differences between the low and high projections are as follows:
1. The amount of per capita consumption increases in all but the top quintile of consumers (see text, pp. 116 and 117).
2. Business investment in plant and equipment, assumed to be 15 percent of aggregate GNP in the high projection, 10 percent in the low.
3. Federal defense expenditures, assumed to average $100 billion a year in the high projection, $50 billion a year in the low.

might go from $10 billion in 1966 to as much as $30 billion in the Year-2000. When we are dealing in trillions, we can ignore it.

The foreign balance, representing (1) cumulative investment overseas, and (2) overseas assistance for development, is another matter. The latter quantity at present is running at a very low figure—less than ⅓ percent of GNP, whereas once it was in the magnitude of 1 percent of GNP. For present purposes, I will assume a goal of 1 percent of GNP for this purpose which would use up approximately $500 billion and allow another $500 billion for foreign investment, for a 4 percent GNP growth rate, and $400 billion each for a 3 percent growth rate.

CONCLUSIONS

The projected GNP in each case falls a bit short of meeting the projected demands of the goals proposed, though they might be met with a 4.5 percent growth rate (which is not out of the question).

The main differences between high and low projections are in the bigger variables—consumption, private investment in plant and equipment, and defense. Consumption accounts for about half the difference between the high and low projections, and private investment and defense for about 25 percent each.

Some of the things which seem highly important to us, like urban infrastructure and state and local government services, turn out to be relatively small in the total, and substantial percentage increases could be had with relatively small diversions from the bigger expenditure items.

Investment, as we have emphasized, is a riddle because we have no way of projecting the amount of investment required to produce for the projected gross national product growth rate. Education, which can be regarded as investment in human beings, is in the same category; we do not know how much the GNP growth rate would be affected by expanding or contracting the education expenditure by, say, a trillion dollars. And finally, some of the so-called consumption expenditures are also in the investments category, notably expenditures on health and other items essential to high productivity.

The consumption item offers the greatest opportunity for diversion; if we pare consumption only a little below the figures projected, all other higher-projection goals can be met within the limits of the 4 percent GNP growth rate. But this presumes that people will be willing to be taxed, and to save, at rates higher than present rates.

Several goals of the urban society in the long run will pay for themselves in increased productivity. An example is the raising of educational levels all along the line, particularly the levels of those who otherwise would be caught in the low-culture, low-income trap. Another has to do with the improvement of the urban environment to make it more economically efficient and more aesthetically attractive. Economic efficiency pays off, almost by definition, and in many instances so does aesthetic quality— people will pay more for homes, travel facilities, and workshops in pleasant surroundings than in unpleasant (in the aesthetically attractive new Seagram Building, rents were 25 percent over rents in other buildings close by).

Some of the bolder notions in urban development now going around, such as developing new towns in town or building new cities outside of established urban centers, would involve no great sums of money over what will be spent in any case, simply because the urban population will continue to grow and to demand better environmental conditions. The essential point is how the growth is planned, organized and directed—not in the additional resources that are necessary to achieve it.

In conclusion, this exercise in political arithmetic demonstrates that resources and productivity growth put restrictions on our golden dreams, but that if we are willing to be patient, to put funds where the payoff is highest, and to foster a greater sense of social responsibility, so that more people begin to weigh social costs as well as monetary returns, we can have the means to create a very high quality urban society. And after that, in the twenty-first century, we are assured that we shall have the science of genetics sufficiently under control to be able to alter people to fit the environment as well as to create environment to fit the people. Perhaps in the future when our stock of fossil fuels and other raw materials has been exhausted, this will be the way out.

NOTES

1. *The Wealth of Nations,* Modern Library Edition, p. lvii.
2. The GNP does include several other items not sold on the market, notably the imputed rental value of owner-occupied dwellings.
3. Lecht's sixteen areas are

1. Consumer expenditures and savings
2. Private plant and equipment
3. Urban development
4. Social welfare
5. Health
6. Education
7. Transportation
8. National defense
9. Housing
10. Research and development
11. Natural resources
12. International aid
13. Space
14. Agriculture
15. Manpower training
16. Area redevelopment

4. The goals are essentially those posed by the President's Commission on National Goals in 1960 (*Goals for Americans:* Prentice-Hall, 1960). *Space* was added subsequently.
5. Actually about 197,000,000.
6. In neoclassical economic systems, the amount spent for consumption and investment were brought into proper proportion, with full employment of resources, by the rate of interest. In the age of Neo Keynes, we know that things are vastly more complicated and the rate of interest less potent than the neoclassical model supposed.
7. The 1960 Census discovered about 11,000,000 dwelling units that were substandard—seriously deficient in one or more respects. How much improvement a 1967 Census would show is uncertain; what we do know is that the rate of housing construction has bumped along during most of the 1960s, and in 1966 fell to the lowest level since 1957.
8. See Seymour Melman, *Our Depleted Society* (New York: Holt, Rinehart & Winston, 1965).
9. Between 1964 and 1966, federal purchases of nonmilitary goods and services, deflated for price changes, rose by 3½ percent while transfers to persons and to state and local governments (also deflated) rose by 18 percent.

# 9 Technology and the Changing Social Order

**Kenneth E. Boulding**

When we look at the larger dynamics of society as it is spread out in human history it is by no means easy to tell where technology leaves off and society begins. The world social system, which I have sometimes called the "sociosphere," consists of all three billion human beings, the knowledge and skills that they possess, the roles that they occupy and the organizations in which they participate, plus the changes in all these things and the actions and interactions, the inputs into and outputs from all these "behavior units," both of commodities and of communications. This is a very large and complex system. We must not forget to include within it also all human artifacts and certain relevant parts of the physical environment. It is not easy to distinguish a part of this system and call it "technology." Technology is certainly much more than the artifacts, the houses, machines, tools, automobiles, etc., which surround people and which people use. It consists also of the skills and habits of people who use these artifacts, for the artifacts themselves are useless unless people know how to use them. In this sense we have to think of the individual human being as himself in large part an artifact, the genetic contribution toward which many have been made by almost completely unskilled labor, but in which the skills and knowledge are largely acquired by processes which themselves involve investment in skill and knowledge. If we think of technology therefore as ways of doing things, it is very hard to draw any line between what is technology and what is society. The two concepts seem almost identical. There is a technology for praying as well as for plowing, for producing poetry as well as producing potatoes, for controlling fears as well as for controlling floods.

Even if we succeed in differentiating, shall we say, material technology from the rest of society it is evident that the inter-actions between the two segments of the social system, that is, between what we have defined as technology and the rest of it, are so intimate and complex that we are still really dealing with a single system. Even if one is the chicken and the other is the egg, it is hard to tell which is which, for they succeed each other with such rapidity that they blur. Society produces technology, technology produces society in an endless mesh of action and interaction.

No matter how we define the technological segment of the social system it is clear that behind all technological and social change is the process of increasing human knowledge. Even the set of human artifacts, what the economist knows as "capital," consists in a very real sense of human knowledge imposed and impressed on the physical world. Every artifact originated in an idea in some human mind. It has been created because of some human skill both in production and in organization. However, artifacts help to produce and increase knowledge just as knowl-edge produces the artifact. The invention of writing, for instance, and the artifacts that permit it, such as clay tablets, papyrus, paper, styluses and pens, permitted the storing of human knowl-edge on a scale previously impossible. With writing, the past can speak to the present and the present to the future, and mankind becomes integrated into a much larger knowledge structure than is possible with merely oral communication. The invention of printing enabled existing written knowledge to be propagated to a much larger portion of the population than previously. The invention of radio and television as McLuhan has suggested makes the world into a single village, or perhaps only into a single mob. As knowledge increases it becomes embodied in artifacts, memory banks of books and libraries, and increased human skills which permit an even more rapid increase. It is this fact of increase leading to still more rapid increase that creates the peculiar dynamic instabilities of social systems and that has created in our day what may be described as a "knowledge explosion."

The progressive increase of knowledge which is so character-istic of social systems, at least beyond a certain point of take-off in the neolithic, represents as it were a gear change in the whole evolutionary process. All evolution, whether biological or social, is a process whereby mutation and selection lead to increasingly complex and improbable structures. It is only stretching the meaning of the word a little to say that as we move from hydrogen to helium, from the large molecule to the virus, from the virus to the cell, or from the cell to the many-celled organisms and from these to the vertebrates and from these to man, there is an increase in knowledge at each step. What is going on in the social system, therefore, is merely an acceleration of the total process of evolution, created by the extraordinary capacity for knowledge of the human nervous system.

We can, if we wish, make a distinction between pure knowl-edge and technology, the former being simply "know-what" and the latter being "know-how." This distinction, however, like that between technology and society itself is arbitrary and not easy to draw and each process leads so much into the other that we again have a chicken-egg blur. Nevertheless, one can perhaps point to a certain watershed in history which I would put about 1860, some would put it perhaps a hundred years earlier, before which the dominating force in technological change was what might be called folk knowledge and folk technology arising out of the practical and ordinary experiences of mankind, and after which the enormous dynamic inherent in the specialized process of increase in scientific knowledge became dominant and pulled technology along behind it.

We can certainly trace in the last 10,000 years, or even before, a slow but accelerating process of improvement in folk tech-nology. The great irreversible step was the domestication of crops and livestock and the invention of agriculture. According to one authority, this increased the average life span from about thirty-two years to thirty-eight. This meant a substantial reduc-tion in the rate of consumption of knowledge by death and hence permitted a slow, steady increase both in technological skill and in an unsystematic but useful folk knowledge of materials, plants, animals, minerals, chemical reactions, and so on. The rise of metallurgy, the development of writing, the so-called urban revolution, involving the rise of cities, all seem to have followed directly from the food surpluses that agriculture permitted. Civilization, especially imperial civilization, indeed may even have been a setback in the sense that it often reduced the average length of life, created a highly stratified society and confined reading and writing to small priestly classes who were often much more interested in the perpetuation of their own privileges than in the extension of knowledge itself. There is a good deal of evidence, for instance, that it was the collapse of the Roman Empire in the West that started off a new surge of improving technology after four hundred years of technological stagnation. The Christian monastic orders seem to have played an important role both in the development and spread of technological improvements. Christianity, by reason of its humble origin among carpenters, fishermen, and tentmakers, undoubtedly raised the status of common labor and of the artisan. Its emphasis on the reality and sacredness of the material world also opened the way for technological improvements. These factors seem to outweigh the impact of the ascetic spirit and the eschatological world view which by themselves would be unfavorable to development.

Constantine seems to have marked the end of the Roman stagnation and the beginning of a long slow improvement in prescientific technology which culminated in the so-called industrial revolution of the eighteenth century. It was only in the West, of course, that Christianity was important. In the same period China had an even more rapid rate of development than Europe, and from about the time of Christ to the sixteenth century China was not only the most developed society technologically but also was the source of many technological exports to the West.

The rise of science as a separate and legitimated subculture eventually introduces a higher gear again into the rate of technological evolution. The significant date here is 1660, the foundation of the Royal Society in London, for it represents the legitimation of the scientific subculture. The eighteenth century saw the early beginnings of the impact of science on technology; the reciprocating steam engine probably owed something to Boyle's Law, although the real theory of the steam engine, that is, thermodynamics, did not come along until 1824, almost one hundred years after the steam engine itself. I am inclined myself to regard the development of the eighteenth century as the culmination of the long growth of folk technology, though one must admit that the successful steam engine was a very great step forward. This represented the first time that man had actually created a source of power instead of simply utilizing the powers of nature around him, as in the water wheel or in the windmill, which, incidentally, came surprisingly late, the first recorded mention being about 1180.

It was not until 1860, however, that science-based technology really began to get under way with the development of the chemical industry, which would have been quite impossible without Dalton and Kekulé. A little later comes the electrical industry, which would have been impossible without Faraday, Ohm, and Clark-Maxwell. An even more striking example, of course, is the nuclear industry, which would have been impossible without Bohr and Einstein. We now seem to be on the edge of an enormous expansion of industries based upon biology, of which the spectacular rise in the productivity of agriculture in the last generation may be only the foretaste.

Rates of development in earlier periods of course cannot be measured exactly and must be in part a matter of speculation. It at least illustrates the enormous order of magnitude of the change through which we are going, to suppose that whereas in the paleolithic period it is doubtful whether knowledge doubled in fifty thousand years, in the neolithic period it may have doubled in two thousand years, in the period of civilization it may have doubled every thousand years or less, and in the modern world in many sciences it doubles every fifteen or twenty-five years. We see this process reflected also in the rise of per capita income, which is closely related to the stock of knowledge. In the paleolithic period it may be doubted whether the per capita income changed at all in a hundred thousand years, if indeed the concept has any meaning. After the invention of agriculture and in the age of civilization it may perhaps have doubled every one to three thousand years. In the eighteenth and early nineteenth centuries in the advanced countries it may have doubled in a hundred years. From 1860 on we are on firmer statistical grounds. In the most rapidly developing countries, such as Sweden, Japan, and the United States, the per capita income doubled every thirty years. In Japan since 1946 the per capita real income has approximately doubled every eight years. By comparison we may note incidentally that it took the United States thirty-five years before 1966 to double its per capita income, but the United States is now rich enough perhaps to be a slowpoke. The change even from the nineteenth to the twentieth century in this regard, however, is highly significant. At the best nineteenth century rates of development the children were twice as rich as the parents. At the Japanese rate of development the children may be six times as rich as the parents, and it is not surprising that in Japan they say that it is not only that the parents cannot understand the children, the sophomores cannot understand the freshmen! Whether society can stand a rate of development so enormous without shaking itself apart still remains to be seen.

Even if we do not separate technology sharply from the rest of society we may distinguish within both technology and society a number of subsystems, each of which has a certain dynamic of its own but each of which also interacts with the others. I am suspicious of any monistic interpretation of history that seeks to argue that any one of these subsystems dominates all the others. Neither material technology, as Marx thought, nor a religious and moral technology, as Max Weber suggested, nor biological, genetic, or racial determinants necessarily dominate the others. We can think of history as a kind of layer cake in which a number of different layers run side by side through time, each with a dynamic of its own, and yet each from time to time profoundly penetrating and interacting with others. One layer, and a very thick layer, is that of material technology, consisting of human artifacts, and the way in which human beings interact with them. This layer has undoubtedly a good deal of independence. We can see, for instance, how the automobile could not have come along much before the end of the nineteenth century because the technological prerequisites were not fulfilled, in the shape, for instance, of rubber technology for the tires, fine machining for the cylinders and pistons, gasoline for the fuel, electrical technology for the spark, and so on. On the other hand, we can also see, especially after the event, that when all these prerequisites have been fulfilled the probability of inventing the automobile was very high indeed. Once the automobile is invented we are not surprised to find a substantial pressure for the improvement of road technology, and we would certainly not be surprised to find a decline of the horse and the horse-based technologies.

Material technology indeed frequently proceeds by a kind of dialectical process with a continuous temporary imbalance in which one invention creates an imbalance in the system in the form of particular scarcities that stimulate another invention to correct the imbalance. The development of spinning and weaving seems to have been an interesting example of this principle. Each improvement in spinning would create a demand for improvement in weaving, and each improvement in weaving would create a demand for improvement in spinning.

Parallel to the development of material technology we have also the development of what might be called social technology. Social artifacts and social inventions are just as real and may be even more important than material artifacts and material inventions. The invention of representative government, for instance, which is a slow process stretching over the centuries, enormously increased the capacity and power of the state and its ability to legitimate its actions. The social invention of the corporation in the eighteenth and nineteenth centuries had an enormous effect on economic development and on the scale of economic organizations without which a great many of the technical developments of the nineteenth and twentieth centuries would have been impossible. Social inventions often have consequences far beyond their intent. A good example of this is the deductible-at-source income tax which was invented almost as a by-product of war finance, but has turned out to be a very powerful social stabilizer, introducing a cybernetic element into the economy that can check both inflation and deflation, especially if the tax is progressive. In an inflation taxes rise currently faster than incomes as people move into the upper brackets which creates government surpluses and checks the inflation; in the case of deflation taxes decline faster than incomes which produces government deficits and stops the deflation. This simple little device may have done more to create the economic success of the post-World War II period than any amount of specific planning.

A very important segment of the stream of social technology which perhaps deserves a label as a subsystem of its own is the stream of ideological and moral invention. Religious and ideological systems tend to have a certain dynamic of their own, following a kind of corruption-reformation cycle. The rise of a new ideology often has profound effects on all other social systems.

These symbolic mutations are virtually impossible to predict and we do not understand very much about what it is even that makes for survival. Why, for instance, did Christianity survive in late Roman times, when Mithraism did not? Why did Islam and the Koran appeal so much to the Arabs and the desert peoples, and Christianity and the Bible appeal more to people in moist temperate climates? How do we account for the extraordinary impact of an almost unreadable book such as Marx's *Kapital* or a curious work like the *Book of Mormon?* How do we account for something like the spectacular rise of Soka Gakki in modern Japan, in which a small obscure sect of Nichiren Buddhism suddenly blooms into a powerful quasi-political organization of three million people! We have to confess, I think, that we know very little about the dynamics of symbolic systems, and we must always be prepared to be surprised by them; that they have a dynamic of their own, however, can hardly be doubted.

Many other subdivisions of the social system could undoubtedly be identified. The three mentioned above, however, which we might perhaps call material technology, social technology, and moral technology, serve to illustrate the complexity of the interaction among the subsystems. The material here is so rich, indeed, that we must content ourselves with a few examples.

An example which is peculiarly relevant to the purposes of this symposium is the close relationship between agricultural technology and the rise of cities. It is only the development of a food surplus from the food producer, made possible by agriculture, that created the conditions for the existence of cities at all. Food surplus alone, however, is not enough. There have been many societies with a food surplus and no cities. The rise of cities demands essentially social inventions, probably indeed moral and ideological inventions. The social invention is the development of political structures of legitimated coercion. These in turn are related closely to the development of religious ideologies to assist in this legitimation. In the age of classical civilization the cities produced very little to exchange for the food that the food producer gives them. Civilization quite literally is founded on agriculture and exploitation. The exploitation, however, is itself a social invention without which the material technology would have quite different results.

The scientific revolution has had an enormous impact on agriculture. The so-called "agricultural revolution"—development of the turnip, of artificial grasses, and the four-course rotation which intertilled crops made possible—began in Western Europe at the end of the seventeenth and beginning of the eighteenth century. Even though this movement, like the "industrial revolution," was also in a way prescientific, it laid the foundation for almost all subsequent development. It increased the food supply, it particularly increased the supply of proteins through better animal feed, it improved animal breeding, it diminished mortality, especially infant mortality, and was perhaps the major factor in the enormous expansion of the northwest European peoples in the following two or three centuries. Here again the technological developments would have been unsuccessful if it had not been for the enclosures, that is, the creation of unified farms, which is really a social invention. As we move into the period of true scientific technology we find a social invention in the United States, the land-grant college, playing an enormous role in the spectacular improvements in agricultural technology of the last hundred years and the subsequent release of a large proportion of the agricultural labor force to manufacturing and to tertiary industries.

It is irresistibly tempting to note a few more examples of the interaction of material and social technology even though they may be a little exaggerated. The stirrup and the rein, for instance, reached Europe after the fall of Rome, almost certainly from China by way of Central Asia. The impact of this apparently simple and obvious invention was enormous. Without it chivalry and the whole apparatus of medieval knighthood would have been much more difficult, for it is hard to have a knight who cannot stay on a horse. The Romans, indeed, could not do anything very energetic on horseback without falling off. A similar connection can be made between the horse collar (which arrived in Europe about the same time, or perhaps a little later) and the great agricultural and building improvements of the tenth and eleventh centuries. The Romanesque and even the Gothic cathedral are a direct outcome of the increased agricultural surplus and draft power that resulted from the horse collar, together, again, with some social inventions, like the three-field system. Eventually, indeed, it has been argued, the horse collar abolished slavery simply because a horse that could pull things was so much better at slave work than a man. The sternpost rudder is another example of what seems like a very obvious invention which came very late. It is first noted in China in the eighth century and in Europe at the end of the twelfth century. It undoubtedly had enormous consequences in enabling ships to travel much longer distances, and it played a great role in the expansion of Europe around the Cape of Good Hope eastward to Asia and across the Atlantic to America. Given a rudder so that he could set a course and steer in a reasonably straight line, it was hard to see how Columbus could miss America.

It is clear that many examples can be cited in which the stream of material technology seems to have been the prime mover in historical development. Other examples can be given, however, as we have seen above, in which social, economic, and political inventions were the prime movers, and led to expansions in material technology. It is hard to evaluate social inventions such as the patent system, but there is little doubt that it has had a marked effect on the acceleration of material invention. Similarly, social inventions such as public education and, in more recent years, organizations like the National Science Foundation are examples where social invention has had enormous consequences on the material world. Man's adventure into outer space, indeed, is a result not of the dynamics of material invention so much as a peculiar dynamic of conflict and emulation between two great powers.

The impact of invention in the moral, religious, ideological, and symbolic sphere is harder to trace, but there can be little doubt that at times it has been enormous. The impact of Islam, for instance, in creating a great civilization within which the scientific achievements of the Greeks were preserved at a time when they might easily have been lost in disorganized Europe undoubtedly advanced technology in the material world. The thesis of Max Weber regarding the impact of Protestantism and especially of Calvinism not only on social inventions such as capitalism but on material inventions which this in turn generated is well known, even if in detail it is open to criticism. The impact of Marxism on the spread of science-based technology has been very substantial even if it has not produced any great innovations in its own right. Further examples could be multiplied, and the principle of mutual interaction of the different levels of technology seems to be secure. Nevertheless the impact or even the very existence of social and moral technologies frequently is unrecognized or at least underestimated, and it can hardly be emphasized too strongly that these stand at least on a par with material technology in the total social process.

In all this complex hurly-burly of interacting systems what do we identify as the "social order" which is supposed to be the second main theme of this essay? Just as we had considerable difficulty in separating technology from the total social system we may find some difficulty in defining the social order in a way that does not take in practically everything. Nevertheless, if we wish to identify a portion of the social system which is particularly relevant to the problem of social order we may perhaps identify a segment of the social system that I have come to call the "integrative system." This is the segment of the social system that deals with such matters as community, identity, status, legitimacy, loyalty, and love. This is a recognizable and identifiable segment of the social system, even though, like all other segments, it shades off into others and is in constant interaction with the other segments. It has, furthermore, a certain inner dynamic of its own, as well as receiving inputs and giving outputs to other systems. The problem of the rise of ideological systems and the social institutions based on them which we have noted above is closely connected with the problem of the dynamics of legitimacy and community. In spite of my previous warnings against making any particular segment of the social system dominant, I find a strong temptation to argue for the dominance of the integrative system over the others, and especially for the dynamics of legitimacy as the key to almost anything else that goes on in social dynamics. The argument is simply that no institution can survive the loss of legitimacy in either of its two major senses, inward legitimacy in the sense of justification on the part of the people who operate the institution, and outward legitimacy or acceptance on the part of the people who constitute its environment. Legitimacy grows slowly and it can collapse quickly. It may be produced by age, by charisma, by appropriate symbolic rhetoric, by linkages with other legitimacies, and also by sacrifice, for we cannot deny the legitimacy of what we make sacrifices for without a threat to our own identity. Legitimacy, however, can collapse very quickly, once

an institution ceases to pay off in some sense. Thus in Europe
the legitimacy of absolute monarchy collapsed, between 1640
and 1920, and the monarchs who survived did so only by aban-
doning their political power and becoming "mere" symbols of
legitimacy. Similarly, in the twentieth century the legitimacy of
empires collapsed. The Reformation, over a large part of Christen-
dom, led to the sudden collapse of the legitimacy of the Pope,
perhaps because he tried to hang on to temporal and spiritual
power too long!

There are interesting questions regarding the technology of
the integrative system as we see it in the organization of religion,
the establishment, and legitimation of the institution of the family,
and the great amount that is invested in the legitimation of the
national state, through education and the public sacrifice of
soldiers. It is interesting to look at political institutions primarily
in terms of the technology of legitimation, although considerations of space make it illegitimate for us to pursue this theme
much further.

What is clear is that there are large mutual interactions between the integrative system in its various aspects and the other
continuing dynamic systems of society. Changes in material technology profoundly affect the integrative system. Thus it seems
plausible to link the development of gunpowder and firearms
with the loss of legitimacy of the feudal baron and the city-state.
The rise of the affluent society and the impact of science-based
material technology has profoundly changed our attitudes toward
the legitimacy of wealth and poverty. Marxism may well have
been propagated by the railroad and destroyed by the automobile. Here again one can only make examples and give sugges-
tions, for the relationships are enormously complex.

In conclusion, can one draw any lessons from what may seem
a rather grandiose argument, for the problem which is the immediate concern of this symposium, which is the future of the city?
The most obvious moral to be drawn from the above argument
is of course that the city must be regarded as a total system.
Today it is unquestionably reeling under the impact of the gallop-
ing dynamic of material technology. The automobile especially
has turned the city inside out and is destroying its center, as
vacant urban-renewal lots in a great many cities testify, and is
turning the ecological pattern of the city from the fan or the

spoked wheel to the doughnut and the loose ring or net structure of ribbon development. The airplane, television, radio are creating the world city, an integrated network of communications based on airports and mass communications, while locally the surrounding tissue decays into ghettos and slums. The need for moral invention is clear. We have here a magnificent example of the principle of disproportion, where inventions in material technology have created an enormous need for balancing inventions in the social and moral order. What these inventions are going to be, however, is hard to predict. Indeed, if we could predict them we could have them now, and there would be no need to invent them!

It is a familiar thesis that one of the major problems of the city arises because it cannot expand its territory into the surrounding suburbs. Hence the central city decays because both its potential leadership and the tax base which that leadership might use in rehabilitation is lost to the central city in the course of the flight to the suburbs. The central city therefore falls back into more and more social disorganization with a vicious cycle of deterioration, further loss of tax base, further flight of leadership outside and so on. I cannot resist quoting a verse on the subject which emerged in my mind at another conference recently:

> The reason why cities are ugly and sad
> Is not that the people within them are bad,
> But that most of the people who really decide
> What goes on in the city live somewhere outside.

It is easy enough to perceive the problem but it is much more difficult to perceive the answer. Do we look, for instance, for an expansion of the city organization into the suburbs and the surrounding territory, to bring back the lost leadership to the city organization as it expands into the greater metropolitan area, like Toronto or Miami? Or do we abandon the concept of the city altogether as wholly inappropriate to the modern world, organize a world city quite self-consciously on a national or even an international basis and then break up the old central cities into twenty or thirty suburbs in the hope of restoring the lost sense of community at the local level for the residual local issues?

All this is highly speculative. It merely points up the fact that in the case of the urban problem we have an example of disproportional development, with material technology having developed such an enormous dynamic that it has created an unusual need for imaginative social and moral technology which in this particular instance seems to be lagging. The question of what philosophical, religious, and ideological framework can sustain the urban world is very intriguing and also very difficult. The great world religions grew up in the age of civilization when on the whole rural life predominated and the city was seen primarily as exploitative. Christianity is a good example of this principle. Its imagery is that of the shepherd and the sheep, the sacrificial lamb, the sower and the seed, the bread and the wine, and though of all the world ideologies it seems to be the one at the moment that is most adaptable and most conscious of the necessity for change, it still does not find it easy to adapt itself to the urban world. Some of the success of communism may perhaps be attributed to the fact that it was born in the British Museum in the middle of the then largest city in the world and that it is urban to the point of being antirural. Its antirural bias, indeed, has been a real handicap to those countries which it dominates, for they have all tried to urbanize on an inadequate rural technological base, and the antirural bias has at least to bear part of the responsibility for the socialist failures in agriculture. Even in America the rural ideology is very strong. Jeffersonian democracy, rural virtue, and the family farm are deep in our political mythology, and our failure to come to grips with the problem of poverty in the cities and of urban disorganization is perhaps a hangover from our rural past. It is at this point that moral invention seems desperately necessary to give hope and significance to a drive in the direction of a better urban world.

I might end therefore on a note of mild economic optimism that where there is a demand there usually eventually develops a supply, and though the principle which I call the principle of fundamental surprise pertains in the prediction of moral invention as in any other, that is, if we could predict it we would have it now, it does not seem unreasonable to look for moral and social inventions in whatever surprising places they may arise as a key to the ongoing development of this urban world. The problem that these inventions have to solve, however, is a tough one and it lies at the heart of a great many of the difficulties of our society. It is a problem fundamentally in the nature of personal identity. In our society it is fairly easy to develop a national identity which is reinforced by the public schools and many other agencies of society. It is fairly easy also to develop what might be called a personal identity in the family, in the small peer group, in the immediate occupational environment, and so on. Many of the problems of the city rise because it requires a strong sense of identity with a community that lies somewhere between the nation and the family or the peer group. This intermediate identity seems very hard to develop, especially in a society as mobile as ours in which people ordinarily do not stay all their lives in the places in which they were born and hence do not develop a strong sense of identity with a particular locality. It may be that there is no answer to this problem at the level of the urban community and that we must seek the answer in a reformation either of the national or personal identities, or maybe both. How this reformation can come about, however, is a mystery which only the future can reveal.

# 10 Man's Debt to Nature: Ecology and the Goals of Urban Development

**Ian L. McHarg**

The simplest way to signify "man's debt to nature" is to break out into a paean of praise to the glories of nature—blue sky and smiling sunlight, moon, stars, ocean and tide, seedtime and harvest, the changing seasons. We can invoke the benign aspects of mountains and rivers, plants and animals, the smiling faces of men, women, and children at work or play in fields and forests. It is all true, but only a part of the story.

Another tack is the more prudent one. Nature is the cornucopia: from this great storehouse comes golden grain, ripe corn, barley, wheat, fruit, and vegetables. Not only these but also valuable and indispensable minerals, iron and coal, oil and gas, limestone and bauxite, gold and diamonds. Hence come the fibers, building materials, cement and brick, glass and wood. Thus is nature seen as commodity.

Still another tack is somewhat more abstract but quite pervasive and as laudatory as the others. Nature is the backdrop to the human play where man plays out his exclusive role with God. Or there is the activist corollary to this, that nature is the arena wherein man will realize himself, making nature over into a human image.

All of these views involve some sense of gratitude to nature and thus some debt; but they also share a detachment from nature. They are views which place man apart from nature at best and in opposition to nature at worst.

My own view is different. It is that man is natural, that there is no nonnature category, that man-nature better defines the relationship in which there is not a "debt" but rather an "obligation." I therefore will address the topic of man in nature, his roles and responsibilities.

In my continuing roles as a teacher, I have sought to persuade to my point of view generations of glossy architects who come from the ends of the earth to study landscape architecture. These men are distinguished, not only by their brilliance, but even more by the unquestioned man-centeredness of their attitude to nature. They are prototypes of those who would make nature into a human image. It becomes clear at the outset that they must be persuaded differently if they are to become landscape architects and assume the responsibility of being the professional conscience of society for the acts of man to nature, the artists who make manifest the natural order within which man exists.

I introduce these students to an experience of my own in order, if not to accomplish this objective, at least to initiate a serious inquiry. Some years ago I encountered a scientist who was engaged in an experiment to send a man off to the moon with the least possible luggage. This experiment involved a simulated capsule that contained a fluorescent tube, simulating the sun. In addition there was a quantity of air, some water, some algae growing in the water together with some decomposer bacteria, and, finally, a man. The experiment was expected to proceed as follows. The algae accomplished photosynthesis through the action of light in the presence of $CO_2$ and water. The plants consumed $CO_2$ and expelled oxygen. The man breathed air, consumed oxygen, and expelled $CO_2$. The algae consumed $CO_2$ and so there was a cycle of oxygen-$CO_2$. The man thirsted and drank some water, he urinated, the plants consumed water, transpired, the condensations were collected and the man drank the water. A closed cycle of water was thus initiated. The man hungered and ate some algae, he defecated; the excrement was reduced by the decomposers and consumed by the algae, enabling it to grow. The man ate some more algae and in this way a closed food cycle was maintained.

Is this the way the world works? Yes, in essential terms, it is. The original energy comes from the sun; the single agent that can transmute this light into being, and thus forms the basis for the biotic food and energy pyramid, is the plant. Man is thus, along with all animals, a plant parasite. Moreover, it is the decomposer organisms that are uniquely capable of reducing the wastes of life and the substance of death and reconstituting these into forms that can be utilized to sustain life. So, in the hierarchy of indispensables there is first the sun, next water, then the atmosphere, and finally plants and decomposers. Such is the world's work, and the principal actors involved.

Now if the man were to remain in the capsule for a long enough period, and the biomass of the algae were equal to that of the man, there is a distinct probability that all the substance that had once been man would be constituted in the algae, all that had been algae would be man. The only difference between them then, in terms of matter, would be the templates of the genetic code. This, it seems to me, gives food for some quiet reflection on the separation of man and nature, and indeed on the claims of the exclusive divinity of man.

There is, in this relationship, no *debt*. The system works by cooperative actions and a division of roles. It is obvious that in this system the great gift of photosynthesis is the beginning. Without this there could be no life. Thereafter the operation depends on the fact that the input of one system is the waste of another. The oxygen wastes of photosynthesis together with the substance of the plant are the input of human metabolism; the wastes of man, reduced by the decomposers, are the input to the plant. And the water goes round and round and round.

The more common view of the world—an exclusive dialogue between men played against the faintly decorative background of nature—is no longer tolerable. It is an infantilism. The sores which men inflict upon the world tissue are now too large and they are beginning to coalesce. We can no longer depend upon the great, silent, unaided regeneration that nature has accomplished in time past to heal man's depradations. There are now too many men, too many sores, and too many assaults to assume that nature itself will include the remedy for man's ignorance, disdain, and malice. We must become preoccupied with nature as process; we must recognize the lesions on the world body and reformulate our view to better approximate reality, to enable us to assume the role of manager of the biosphere.

If this knowledge is necessary for survival and for the realization of man's potential, where do we turn for the essential knowledge of nature and her processes? Where else but to the natural sciences, for there reposes our understanding of the phenomenal world. If we would know of the interactions of organisms and environment, which includes other organisms, where else to turn but to the ecologist, for that is his competence. Moreover, if we would know of the nature of man, then it might be well to heed the ethologists who bring the ecological view to the subject of animal behavior or to the ethnographers who bring the same preoccupation with synthesis to the study of simpler peoples.

The physical scientists bring evidence of laws in operation for over four billion years; the life scientists bring evidence of only a billion years less. The ecologists are concerned with the responses of organisms and environment over this long period, while the ethologists study animal behavior encompassing the entire evolutionary journey. In this scale the history of man is brief indeed, and our perception of him can only be enlarged by an understanding of physical and biological laws and the entire sweep of evolution.

For that man who gives form to change, be it for a region or a garden, for space or buildings, the science of ecology is an indispensable perception. It is more; the insights it contains provide a license to intervene with intelligence and give form to the land. In its absence, caprice and arbitrariness rule.

The theoretical basis for ecology has been stated elsewhere and it should suffice here to abstract a workman's code from this science. But first, it is necessary to affirm that the sum of the earth's evolution has been creative and that we, with all the world's denizens, are involved in the future of this creative process. The early sterile world was racked with vulcanism on its first stages toward equilibrium. The modern world, much more stable, contains life—myriads of creatures, fulfilling roles, united in cooperative arrangements. The earliest stages have not been superseded but augmented—representing the sum of creation.

Henderson assured us that the world was fit and could be made more fitting. Darwin assured us that the surviving organism was fit for the environment and that evolution proceeded through natural selection by way of mutation. The environment is fit; the organism is fit for the environment. Evolution has proceeded by increasing the fit, by the essential adaptation between the organism and the environment. This, then, is the task of those who seek to plan and to build.

In the beginning, the sun fell upon a sterile earth and the energy gained equaled that which was lost. Today, the same energy powers the inert and living world, transmuted through plant photosynthesis, utilized by animals, with matter recycled by the decomposers. These creatures, successively more complex as they rise in the phylogenetic scale, represent, in their beings and the orderings which they and their antecedents have accomplished, the sum of creation. Creation is seen then as the entrapment of energy and its employment with matter for an increase in order, which is to say, negentropy (negative entropy). The bulk of this work is accomplished by the smallest and simplest plants and animals. Man has little role.

When energy is considered as information and apperception as a measure of the capacity to transform information into meaning, however, man is seen to be superbly endowed. The value of apperception lies in the capacity to create those cooperative arrangements that are beneficial. It is these that have made possible the evolution to the cell, the organ, organism, and the community. Apperception is, then, the key to symbioses, those beneficial cooperative mechanisms which Selye describes as altruism. The measure of fitness includes the capacity to create cooperative arrangements with other creatures, which involves adaptations to the environment. It is in this sense that man may employ his unique apperception to manage the biosphere.

Creation, therefore, consists of utilizing energy to raise matter into successively higher levels of order, and symbiosis is revealed as an essential ingredient in this process. Evolution is creative; destruction, the reduction to lower levels of order, is retrogressive.

Evolution has proceeded from simple to complex, from unicellular to multicellular, from a few species to many. Multiply simplicities and uniformities result; the multiplication of complexities produces diversities. Complexity results in and from an increase in the number of species. As these increase, they perform more roles and utilize more energy pathways, with a resultant increase in the conservation of energy which in turn reveals low entropy. In summary, creation and evolution reveal a set of attributes that are in opposition to those of destruction and retrogression, as indicated in the following diagram.

| retrogression | evolution |
|---|---|
| ← | → |
| simple | complex |
| uniformity | diversity |
| instability | stability (steady-state) |
| low number of species | high number of species |
| high entropy | low entropy |
| independence | interdependence (symbioses) |

There is one other attribute that may subsume creation and its attributes: that is health. Dr. Luna Leopold offers an example of health in a physical process. He is able to describe a duration curve for a stream. When the stream oscillates above or below this curve, as in a flood or drought, it is in disequilibrium and may be described as unhealthy. Streams normally evolve toward equilibrium which, in this sense, would be described as health.

For living systems Dr. Ruth Patrick has developed stream biological profiles which reveal the number of aquatic species. Health is measured by the degree to which the number of species present approaches the maximum; a decline in the number of species is evidence of ill health. Although the evidence is less than complete for terrestrial systems, and is complicated by the fact that the climax often contains less than the maximum number of species, there is an increasing presumption that the same condition applies to terrestrial ecosystems.

This conception of health, if correct, would subsume fitness, creation, and all the other attributes of this state. In contrast, pathology, or a condition of less than health, would reveal unfitness and both destructive and retrogressive attributes.

For those who are concerned with form, the most important proposition is that form and process are indivisible aspects of the single phenomenon of "being." Furthermore, process can be measured in terms of creation or destruction. That process which is creative, be it a cell, organ, organism, or community, by definition will be fit and will reveal its fitness in form. If the model is correct, it will also be healthy. Show me an environment of health, therefore—physical, mental, and social—and I will show you a community that is fit as revealed in the form of its creatures, their symbiotic relations, and in the environment that they have selected and adapted. In contrast, an environment of pathology will exist where the creatures are unfit, unhealthy, retrogressing, and this too will be revealed in form. This is a conclusion of unimaginable importance to those who are concerned with the physical and social environment.

From this model several important additional conclusions can be derived. The first is that there is, for every place in the world, a "most fit" community of creatures. The second is that there must be a fit community for man, but this presumably will vary from place to place, depending on the nature of the environment. The third conclusion is that creativity, fitness, and health will be revealed inescapably in form. This conception thus becomes of value for both diagnosis and prescription. First, however, we must have much more knowledge about the components of the physical and social environments that contribute to health and disease—that are fit or unfit, creative or destructive—and their formal implications.

The foregoing small segment of ecological theory has been presented in an enormously simplified way, but it can be seen that it offers an unequaled perception for those preoccupied with the environment. This perception can be summarized very generally in the following way. Nature is *process;* it contains values and opportunities for human use, but it also reveals constraints and even prohibitions. Nature reveals past and present processes in *form.* Indeed, in Norbert Weiner's phrase, the world consists of "To Whom It May Concern" messages—but these are clothed in form. Every place is "because," and it reveals in its form the sequence of past processes that contributed to the present reality. Each place and its creatures not only contain values for man but also implications for both his functions and his forms. This view is essential for the person who would intervene in nature with intelligence, to say nothing of an aspiration for art.

It is clear that society at large does *not* view nature in this way, and the lesions on the land are the proof. Let me cite my neighboring state of New Jersey, for example, where there is much conspicuous evidence of this: the treatment of the New Jersey Shore is certainly among the most blatant; the management of the Delaware River is one more; the location of highways in the state is a further example; and the squalor of urbanization which is represented by the extension of the New York metropolis is, perhaps, the most scabrous urban concentration in the entire country.

Space limitations exclude preoccupation with this last example, though it would be interesting to speculate on this urban wen in terms of urban pathology or health. Each of the other examples also represents a clear abuse of nature as value, opportunity, or constraint, and clearly could be discussed in terms of the roles and responsibilities of man. Certainly the most conspicuous example of ignorance and irresponsibility, however, is the abuse of the New Jersey Shore—which I shall now develop in some detail for purposes of exposition of the ecological approach.

The precipitous faces of the Hudson and Hatteras canyons and the Blake Escarpment rise from the abysmal oceanic plain of the Atlantic to the Continental Shelf, and it is upon this that there exists a string of sand bars from Massachusetts to Florida, a part of which is the New Jersey Shore. While Cape Cod is essentially a terminal moraine with outwash plains (the residue from the Buzzard's Bay and Cape Cod ice lobes of the last glaciation), and the Florida Keys are old coral reefs, the sand bars that parallel New Jersey and reach south of Cape Hatteras have more recent origins.

It seems that the processes that determine the creation of sand bars are under the control of waves and wind. Storm waves breaking in relatively deep water offshore cause the erosion of a trough in the sand and the deposition of a low submarine bar near and parallel to the shore. When this process continues, raising the bar above the water level, a dune is formed which is immediately affected by wind processes. An angle of between five and ten degrees on the ocean floor is associated with bar and subsequent dune formation. These emerge and coalesce as a continuous dune. The area of water between dune and shore becomes a shallow lagoon or bay.

Ensuing dune formation then occurs on the seaward side where an offshore submarine bar is formed which subsequently rises above the sea. The intervening area between the two dunes is filled with sand by the wind and the result typically is the following cross-section: beginning with the ocean, there is the intertidal zone, the beach, and the primary dune (primary in defense but secondary in time); behind this is a trough that rises to the inland dune which in turn falls from the back dune to the flat zone, terminating in the bayshore and the bay.

Such a cross-section reveals a number of environments, and their variations are vividly reflected in plant ecology. Perhaps the most stringent factor is salinity, particularly as contributed by salt spray. The lagoon is likely to be brackish and this too is an important limiting factor. As oil floats on water, so does fresh water float on salt water. There is then a prism of fresh water within the dune but it responds to tides and rises and falls twice each day. This decline in water level will be more serious on the dunes than in the trough or the bayshore. The problem of onshore winds combined with salt spray is yet another environmental factor. As a consequence the foredune will be more exposed than the backdune; the sheltered trough and back of the inland dune will offer the most protected locations. In response to these, plants occupy selected locations and create a mosaic of associations. But they are all responsive to the onshore wind with its attendant sea spray, and thus the tips of the tallest plants conform to the parabola of the wind initiated by the primary dune.

As the dune begins to form, the marram grasses colonize it and enhance its growth by arresting grains of sand. From the bayshore, the pioneer is reed grass. Dune formation assumes the form of a continuous ridge on which the marrams spread. Sea myrtle arises seaward of the reed grass on the bayshore. A trough is formed in advance of the initial dune which leads to the formation of the primary dune. This is colonized by dune grasses which accelerate its formation and stabilization. Beach heather volunteers among the dune grass; blueberry and beach plum extend from the bayshore toward the backdune. As the primary dune grows, a dune grass savannah develops in the trough; the marram and the beach heather consolidate the original dune, while woody plant material, notably red cedar, grows in the backdune and poison ivy joins the blueberries near the bayshore. In the final stage the beach remains devoid of vegetation, but on the primary dune is a thick stand of dune grass, while in the trough there are low myrtle, beach plum, and smilax thickets which have replaced the grass. The face of the inland dune is covered by beach plum and parthenocisus, interspersed with grass, while in the backdune there is a red cedar-pine woodland that graduates into a swampy red cedar woodland and thence to the reed grass and the thistle, Baccharis, and to the bay.

We can draw several conclusions from this simple description and analysis of the ecology of the New Jersey Shore. The first is that the sand dune is a very recent formation, unlike the Coastal Plain formed in Tertiary and Cretaceous times, or the Piedmont half a billion years old in the Cambrian era. It will change in configuration in response to autumn hurricanes and winter storms. The dune is likely to be breeched under these conditions and an examination of air photographs shows quite different water channels and land formations. During storms the bay is likely to fill and flood the bayshore and trough. In severe winter storms the sea may cross over the entire sand bar. This is a consideration of some importance—the New Jersey Shore is not a certain land mass like the Piedmont; it is still involved in a contest with the sea; its shape is dynamic.

The next conclusion is that its relative stability is dependent upon the anchoring vegetation. There are several distinct lines of concern from this point. The first involves ground water. If the use of wells lowers ground water below a critical level, the stabilizing plants will die. On the other hand, if by the building of groins or any other tangential construction the littoral drift is arrested, the source of sand to supplement the dunes will be denied. The final point is that this critical vegetation, the dune grass, is most vunerable to trampling.

We now have a code of basic prohibitions for human use. *Thou shalt not walk on the dune grasses. Thou shalt not lower ground water below the critical level. Thou shalt not interrupt littoral drift.* These proscriptions merely will ensure the perpetuation of a natural sand bar and its native vegetation and expression. This merely will sustain a public resource. We must now consider the matter of the people who would like to develop this resource. What can we say to them?

Perhaps the most reasonable approach would be to investigate the tolerance or intolerance of the various environments to human use in general and to certain particular uses which are common in this area. The first zone is the beach and, fortunately for us all, it is astonishingly tolerant. It is cleaned by the tides twice a day of the debris that men leave and even the most vulgar residues achieve a beauty when handled by the sea. The creatures that live in this area do so mostly in the sand and thus escape destruction from humans. So the beach is tolerant to all the happiest of uses: swimming and picnicking, the making of sandcastles, fishing, and sunbathing.

The next zone, the primary dune, is totally different—it is absolutely intolerant. It cannot stand any trampling; it must be prohibited to use. If it is to be crossed, and crossed it must be to reach the beach, then this must be accomplished by bridges. Moreover, if the dune is to offer defense against storms and floods then it must not be breeched. No development should be permitted on the primary dune, therefore, no walking should be allowed, and it should not be breeched at any point.

The trough is much more tolerant; development can occur there. It is more protected than the dune, of course, from storms, wind, and blowing sand. The problem is ground water. The vegetation that occupies this zone exists because of the relative abundance of fresh water. Should this water level be lowered, the stabilizing vegetation will die. Lowering can be accomplished through withdrawals from wells, but it also will result from roofs and paving that divert runoff into drains and from piped waste-water systems.

The inland dune is the second line of defense and is as vulnerable as the primary dune. It too is intolerant and should not be developed. The backdune however reveals a more permissive location and is perhaps the most suitable environment on the sand bar for man. Normally it supports woody vegetation, red cedar and pine. The shade of these trees is a welcome relief from the blinding light, glare, and heat which characterize all the other zones. Fresh water is more abundant in this environment than the others, an important consideration for development.

The final zone is the bay. It is not well known that estuarine and bayshore environments are among the most productive in the world, exceeding even those better-known examples of rice paddies and sugar cane farms. It is in these nutrient, rich locations that the infantile stage of most of the important fish takes place and where dwell the most valuable shellfish; they are also the breeding grounds and homes of the most important wildfowl. In our society it would appear that there is an implicit law which enjoins all disposers of rubbish and garbage, all those who would gratify their heart's desire by filling land, to choose marshes and bayshores for their gratification. This reveals a profound ignorance about the values of nature; the marshes and bays are among the most productive areas that we have. *Thou shalt not fill or dump in marshes and bays.*

It takes only the shortest of reflection to realize that those environments which support aquatic and semiaquatic vegetation normally are occupied by, or adjacent to, water. Indeed, distance from water is one of the most precise divisions of plant associations. Knowing this, it is not difficult to determine which environments are owned by water and which are not. If the eel grass flats on either side of the bayshore are filled, in disregard of this determination, it is clear that the capacity of the bay to contain water will be reduced. We can assume that winter storms and hurricanes will continue with their normal frequency, but the water storage capacity of the lagoon will have been diminished. The water will then occupy that area that it requires, inevitably covering the prior area now occupied by building. Moreover, in the process of filling and building, it is likely that erosion will have tended to fill the lagoon, making it more shallow and reducing its storm water capacity still further. This will lead to an even larger area of built-up land being inundated in any storm.

We can say, therefore, that if you wish to find a location that is likely to be flooded, by all means fill in the marsh on either side of the bay and build there. If you wish to make this flooding a certainty, then fill the lagoon with sediments. In addition, you will also have the assurance of the least stable foundations. Consistency is not a very noble virtue, but it is the only one in this sad catalogue of actions. Surely, this is not the way to act. Let us say rather that marshes were not made to be filled; they constitute a real value in their natural state and a real danger to human habitation. *Thou shalt not develop marshes.*

But in the search for a suitable environment for man, we have disclosed a most fortunate situation. The width of a dune tends to be a function of its height and the angle of repose of stabilized sand, and therefore it does not occupy much space. The backdune area tends to be the largest of all of the components of the sand bar, however, and it is here, propitiously, that the most delightful, rich, safe, and tolerant environment for man exists.

On the basis of this sketchy knowledge of ecology we can now consider positive recommendations for the development of shore area resources. The place where the backdune is widest would appear to offer the maximum opportunity for the concentration of facilities, be it a village, a group of houses, or a recreational center. There will be located, of necessity, a highway. It will inevitably run parallel to the sea and the dunes, and, if sufficiently elevated, it could not only proffer splendid views of the ocean and the beach, but it could provide a third dune, the equivalent of the Dutch Sleeper (final defense against the sea). If development were limited to the bayshore side of this backdune, it would offer protection from winter storms, and could prevent the breeching of the sand bar from the bayshore, as has happened in the past. But in creating works like an artificial dune to support a highway, it is important that the sand be withdrawn from the ocean and not from the bay. The beach is not a very rich environment, while the bay is the very richest. As Dr. Stanley Cain has revealed, dredging of such rich environments can produce biological deserts.

Development should not occur on the narrowest sections of the sand bar, for that is where breeching is most likely. Now if communities are established, there arises the problems of water supply and sewage disposal. First, the matter of water: there are resources of ground water in the sand bars, as we have seen, but the water level must not be lowered to such a level as will extinguish the stabilizing vegetation. This suggests that a number of wells be located to distribute the withdrawals; but water from this source will be a limiting factor to growth. Sewage represents another problem: the silts of the bayshore are unsuitable for septic tanks and, moreover, the employment of this technique is certain to pollute the ground water supply. A sewage treatment plant will be necessary before development is permitted.

We now have the broad outlines of an ecological analysis and a planning prescription based upon this understanding. A spinal road would constitute a barrier dune and be located in the backdune area. It could contain all utilities, water, sewer, telephone, electricity, and would be the guardian defense against flood. At the widest points of the backdune, communities of human settlement would be located. Development should be excluded from the vulnerable, narrow sections of the sand bar.

The bayshore would be, in principle, left inviolate. The beach would be available for the most intensive use, but with no building. Approaches to it would be by bridges across the dunes which, in turn, would be prohibited to use. Limited development would be permitted in the trough, determined by ground water withdrawals and the effect upon vegetation. A positive policy would suggest accelerating the stabilizing processes, both of dune formation and of vegetative growth. To do this, vegetation appropriate for each association would be planted. Particular attention would be given to marram grasses on dunes, and to the provision of red cedars and pines on the backdune.

In the Netherlands, confronted with a similar situation, it became a matter of national resolve to reclaim land from the sea and a positive policy was developed toward that end. If this were applied to the New Jersey Shore, it would involve the creation of continuous dikes and dunes facing the sea. There would be locks at those locations where the lagoon was connected to the ocean. Fresh water flow from the land mass into the bay would be regulated, as would incursions of salt water from the ocean. Constraints would be exercised to maintain dunes and dikes, ground water withdrawals, and native vegetation.

Sadly, no such planning principles have been developed in New Jersey. While all of the ecological principles are well known to botanists and ecologists, this had no effect whatsoever upon the form of development. Houses are built upon dunes, grasses destroyed, dunes breached for beach access, ground water withdrawn with little control, areas paved, and bayshores filled and built upon. Ignorance is compounded with anarchy and greed to make the raddled face of the Jersey Shore.

From the fifth to the eighth of March, 1962, there came retribution. A violent storm lashed the entire northeast coast from Georgia to Long Island. For three days sixty mile an hour winds whipped the high spring tides across a thousand miles of ocean. Forty-foot waves pounded the shore, breached the dunes, and filled the bay which in turn spilled back across the islands to the ocean. When the storm subsided, the extent of the disaster was revealed. Three days of storm had produced, in New Jersey alone, eighty million dollars' worth of damage: twenty-four hundred houses destroyed or damaged beyond repair and eighty-three hundred houses partially damaged; several people killed and many injured; roads and utilities destroyed. Fire subsequently added to this destruction. The damages were compounded for the majority of people because there was little recoverable by insurance. Many people are still making mortgage payments on houses that were bulldozed into the bay. There were other significant losses, of course, not the least of which was the loss of income from tourism which is the major economic base of the New Jersey Shore. In addition, this place, thought to be a recreational resource for the region, looked a sorry mess. Yet all of this disaster was caused by man, through sins of commission and omission!

Immediately after the disaster giant bulldozers pushed the wrecked houses into the bay, or burned them in great funeral pyres; sand dunes were reformed, streets exhumed from under the overburden of sand; and slowly, houses reappeared to fill the sites of those which had been swept away. The most common problem was the exposure of foundations—those houses which had sat high on the dune, commanding the sea, found the sand swept from under them and there they stood, floors fifteen feet above the sand, grotesquely leaning, supported on their exposed telegraph pole foundations. But not all of them: in a remarkable example of wisdom and virtue rewarded, the houses endured in those rare cases where the dune was stable and unbreeched, clothed in grasses, though they suffered the minor problems of broken windows and lost shingles.

The evidence is there to be read. The record of cause and effect constitutes the common knowledge of many natural scientists. But the *status quo ante* is being reconstituted without direction or constraint. The future seems clear—the New Jersey Shore lies in the path of hurricanes and can expect the attendant storms; winter storms are even more regular. Sand bars are recent and ephemeral and there is no assurance that they will endure. There is no reason to believe that the last storm was the worst. In the Netherlands, it was a "thousand year storm" that took almost two thousand lives and caused untold damage, all but inundating this best prepared of all people. What can the most unprepared people of New Jersey expect? We hope for the best, but it would be sanguine to expect anything less than disaster. This is what is being invited . . . again.

In the past, unusually perceptive planners and designers have been able to create adaptations which are, indeed, fit and which demonstrate this in their form. Yet this has not developed from principle and so the intuitive professionals are seldom able to transmit to colleagues or students the bases for their rare successes. The particular value of the ecological view is that it permits adaptations by man to be scrutinized and examined against the criteria that hold for all physical and biological processes. Moreover, for the first time there is the promise that these vital subjects—creativity, health, fitness—which have heretofore been considered subjective, may be incorporated into regional and city planning, landscape architecture, and architecture. In this model, creation and destruction, health and disease, fitness and unfitness, appear to be facets of two extreme conditions. And they are inescapably linked to form.

If this is so, there is the promise of an emergent body of principles for those concerned with molding the physical and social environment; and with this, the professional can rise to a new relevance. Even more important is the possibility of a union of science and art in which the natural and social scientists, together with the medical professionals, can unite with the planners and designers to create environments of health, creativity, and fitness, revealed in form.

If this is the objective, then ecology is indispensable for its realization. Yet the acceptance of the ecological view of man-nature is not only indispensable to those who are concerned with conscious adaptations of the land; it is equally important to society in general. If man does have a debt to nature then it is indicated by his obligation to understand nature as an interacting process which in sum has been creative. It is essential that we know of the evolutionary past, the major actors who perform the world's work, the elements of creativity and its attributes, and that we see from this that nature is a value system which offers opportunities for human use, but just as clearly presents constraints and prohibitions. When this is understood, and land use and management reflect such understanding, then we shall see the morphology of man-nature in both city and countryside. Here there will be no debt, but the expression of man, a natural being, using his consciousness to manage the biosphere.

# 11 Western Man's Search for a New Sociocultural Home

**(A Prognosis of the Sociocultural Shape of the Western World in This and the Twenty-First Centuries)**

**Pitirim A. Sorokin**

A. THE BASIC ASSUMPTIONS OF THE PROGNOSIS

I shall begin my prognosis with an enumeration of the assumptions under which it may be correct:

1. The first of these assumptions is that so long as human history remains *creative,* as hitherto it has been in many of its periods, no accurate scientific prediction of the future sociocultural state of mankind or of its industrialized, urbanized and technologically advanced societies is possible. This is because the very concept of creativity implies something new, unforeseen, unknown before, and therefore unpredictable.[1]

Predictions concerning historical trends have a real chance to be correct only when restricted to the routine, frequently repeated, uncreative aspects of history, and then only for a limited time and under specified conditions. I am assuming that the historical life of humanity and of Western societies will remain creative in many fields of personal, social, and cultural life in this and the next centuries.

2. Besides this factor of creativity there is another factor which greatly increases the difficulty of a correct prediction of the future shape of sociocultural organization and historical processes. It consists of the great complexity and contradictory tendencies that exist in today's world.

These two assumptions explain why I prefer to call these prognoses "guesses" instead of "scientific predictions." I hope, however, that these "guesses" may be as "lucky" as most of my "prognostications" made in the nineteen twenties and thirties.[2]

3. I assume further that during the period under discussion *there will not be any new world war* (though in my opinion the chances of our escaping such a war are only slightly better than fifty–fifty). The reason for this assumption is obvious: if a new world war explodes, it will certainly terminate for a long time the creative mission of man on this planet. In such a condition there would be no need for scientific predictions about the shape of human affairs to come. There probably would not be any group left to read scientific treatises on this or any other topic. In that case a memorial *Requiem Aeternam* would be more proper if any group survives that is capable of performing the memorial service and singing the *Requiem.*

4. I assume also that the existing rate of increase of human population on this planet will be notably slower than it is now, and that the total size of the human race in the twenty-first century will not exceed some five to six billion people. Population increase beyond this size would necessitate a considerable change of my prognoses.

5. My next assumption is that the creative leadership of mankind which has been monopolistically centered in the West for the last four centuries will continue to expand and diffuse to include the peoples of Asia, Africa, and Latin America, and that the unification of mankind into *one interdependent whole* will continue to increase. These trends are already going on and should continue.[3] Though subsequently I shall be discussing mainly Western industrialized and urbanized societies, my prognoses in a modified form aim to be applicable not only to the West but to the East also.[4]

6. Finally I assume that my diagnosis of the *present* state of the Western world and mankind—developed in my main works—is roughly correct.[5] A brief sketch of this state follows.

### B. THE PRESENT STATE OF WESTERN URBANIZED, INDUSTRIALIZED, AND TECHNOLOGICALLY ADVANCED SOCIETIES

As early as the nineteen twenties I diagnosed the present state of Western technologically advanced societies as a *most critical transitory state from a disintegrating Sensate or Secular—cultural, social, and personal—order that has been dominant during the last five centuries or so to a new order which is not yet built and remains little known in its essential features.* This dominant

Sensate order is built upon a major premise or postulate that true reality and value are sensory, that beyond what we can see, hear, taste, and perceive through our senses and with their extensions—microscopes, telescopes, radar, etc.—there is no reality and no value. Sensate society and culture articulate and "materialize" this ultimate premise in their main institutions, in their system of values, in their science and philosophy, in their modicum of religion, in their law and ethics, fine arts, politics and economics, in the dominant mentality and conduct of their members, and in the dominant ways of life.

In the history of the European sociocultural world this Sensate order emerged in the twelfth century, and about the end of the fifteenth century it became the dominant order in the Western world. During its domination it delivered to mankind magnificent achievements in science and technology, in philosophy and Sensate fine arts, in Sensate ethics and law, economics and politics. About the end of the nineteenth century it began to disintegrate and in the twentieth century it largely crumbled. By this crumbling it ushered the West and mankind into a most critical transitory passage toward a new order not yet built.

The Sensate order replaced the quite different Ideational or Religious order which was dominant in the Middle Ages. The Ideational order of the Middle Ages was based upon a quite different ultimate postulate, namely that *the true reality and value is God and God's Kingdom* as they are described in the Bible, and defined in the Christian *Credo*. The Medieval Ideational sociocultural world articulated and "materialized" this principle in all the main compartments of its culture and social life and in the dominant mentality and conduct of its populations. Having delivered its great values in religion, philosophy, theology, Ideational fine arts, ethics and law, economics and politics, during the centuries of its domination (from the sixth to the end of the twelfth) this Religious-Ideational order began a decline that continued up to recent times.

Concurrent with the onset of the decline of the Ideational order, Sensate premises and order emerged and began to grow. These declining and growing streams of Ideational and Sensate orders met, blended together, and produced a magnificent *Integral* order dominant during the thirteenth and fourteenth centuries. The Integral order is based upon a different ultimate principle, namely that *true reality and value is an infinite manifold, partly sensory, partly rational, and partly supersensory, all unified harmoniously in the infinite God and God's* summum bonum. In contrast to the Ideational postulate this Integral premise did not deny the reality and value of sensory and rational dimensions, and in contrast to the postulate of Sensate order it did not reduce the reality and value of the infinite, total manifold to a merely sensory dimension. It clearly asserted that besides the sensory form of reality-value there are rational and super-sensory-superrational (but not supernatural) forms. In the thirteenth and fourteenth centuries the highest and central features of the social, cultural, and personal orders of the European world articulated and objectified this postulate.

Such in a very sketchy way is the meaning of Sensate, Ideational, and Integral sociocultural orders and the succession of their domination in the history of the Western world. The previously mentioned collapse of the Sensate order in the twentieth century has brought the whole Western world to a state of greatest crisis, perhaps *the* greatest in all human history. The crisis involves all areas of Western society and culture, the whole mentality and behavior of Western peoples, their system of values and their way of life. In this sense the crisis is total, epochal, and infinitely greater than many other crises involving only part of Sensate institutions, values, and sociocultural realities: political, economic, moral, legal, aesthetic, religious, philosophical, scientific, and technological.

One of the major results of this total crisis has been this century's gigantic explosion of international and civil wars, of bloody revolutions and conflicts, and of the worst forms of violence characterizing the relationships among individuals and groups. Our investigation of the movements of wars and important internal disturbances in the history of Ancient Greece and Rome and of the main European countries has shown that the twentieth century is the bloodiest and the most turbulent century of all the twenty-five centuries of Greco-Roman and Western history.[6] If and when persons and groups cease to be controlled in their behavior and relationships by deeply internalized moral precepts of religion or by secular and rational norms of "humanistic" and utilitarian-hedonistic ethical and legal commandments they inevitably become controlled by rude force assisted by fraud.

The collapse of Sensate ethical values has engendered precisely this sort of wholesale demoralization which in its turn produced the extraordinary explosion of the Hobbesian *bellum omnium contra omnes* in our time.

This total crisis is at the root of the much-discussed crises and struggles of capitalism vs. communism, democracy vs. autocracy, freedom vs. regimentation, religion vs. atheism and agnosticism, materialism vs. idealism, "classic" art vs. "modern" art, "new morality" vs. "traditional" morality, and so on. All these crises and struggles are but a partial manifestation of the total collapse of the Sensate sociocultural order. As a result of this collapse proud Western man has found himself bewildered and confused among the debris of his magnificent Sensate home, while a new home has not yet been built. Western man right now is trying to build this new home containing a new sociocultural order, but so far he has not made very much progress. To date he has been able only to clean up part of the old debris and to design part of the new foundation. But even this design is still unclear, and in his mind and heart a struggle is going on between the desire to rebuild the crumbled Sensate home and the yearning to build a new one quite different from the Sensate pattern. In larger terms this signifies a sociocultural struggle between remnants of the Sensate order and a new order which is barely emerging. Today this struggle is going on in science, philosophy, religion, ethics, law, fine arts, politics, and economics. It also is going on in the minds and hearts of every one of us.[7]

In a sketchy way such is my diagnosis of the present state of Western society, culture, and man.

## C. A PROGNOSIS OF THE INTEGRAL ORDER TO COME

Having outlined the assumptions of my prognoses and the present state of the Western sociocultural world, I can now venture to offer several sociocultural prognoses about the shape of Western societies to come. These prognoses concern only the basic dominant order and other essential characteristics of the Western human universe and not its details, however interesting they may be.

Since I assumed hypothetically that there would be no new world war, it follows that the highly urbanized, industrialized, and technologically advanced societies of the West will continue to live and function. For possibly as much as a century ahead their life course is likely to be in a messy transitional state from the dying Sensate order to a new one which will slowly emerge. This transitory period will continue to be marked by the now familiar confusion of values, beliefs, and aspirations; by moral, mental, aesthetic, and cultural anarchy; and by an abundance of interpersonal and intergroup conflicts that have been inherent in, and typical of, all the periods of great transition from one basic dominant order to a different one.

The United States and other Western countries in the decades ahead will probably witness a growth of Caesarism (in Spengler's terms), governmental compulsory regimentation, and "Pentagon totalitarianism"; a decline of genuine free enterprise and capitalist economy, and of individual freedoms; an increase in crime, neurosis and psychosis, suicide, and several forms of morbidity; a decrease of vital, mental, moral, and economic well-being; and a further disintegration of the family and other basic institutions, particularly those that are characteristic of genuine democracy. All of this will be accompanied by an upsurge of intergroup conflict and violent internal disturbances. Despite an enormously increased use of tranquilizers, a spirit of restlessness and lack of peace of mind and happiness will be widely prevalent. Eventually this confusion, anarchy, anomie, and conflict must subside, however, if Western societies are to be capable of building a new and great sociocultural order (as we assumed they would, though the assumption itself is purely hypothetical).

The reasons for this prediction of so long a transitory period are several. First, in all past transitions from Sensate to Ideational or Integral orders, or from one of these to Sensate, a time span of some 150 to 250 years was needed to accomplish the transition. Perhaps in our "modern age" this span can be somewhat shortened, but hardly more than to a period of two or three "generations" of some thirty years each.[8] Second, the state of today's Western human population and of its leaders and power elites hardly warrants an expectation of a much shorter time period necessary for their mental, moral, and sociocultural transformation and the establishment of a new order. This population and its predominantly Sensate power elites cannot be changed basically in one generation. They are deeply engaged in overkill wars and a Hobbesian "war of each against all" (despite their lip service to the highest values and to God); greatly preoccupied with a ferocious struggle for existence and with getting the greatest possible share of wealth, power, and pleasure; powerfully led by morally nihilistic governments anxious to incinerate the whole human race for the realization of their selfish Lilliputian ambitions; and strongly preferring a mess of vulgar cultural pseudo-values in fine arts, ideologies, and recreation. Two or three generations, at least, are needed to transform a contemporary Sensate man into an Ideational or Integral person. So much for the prognosis of *the length of the transitory period.*

The next guess concerns *the kind of new order which may emerge with the termination of the great transition.* Will it be a revived and reinvigorated Sensate order which most of the power elites seem to be anxious to rebuild? Will it be a new variation of either the Ideational or Integral orders? Or, will it be perhaps some sort of eclectic conglomeration of all kinds of social, cultural, and personal values, systems, relationships, and institutions coexisting with one another but free from unity and consistency?

My guess is that at the present juncture of human history nobody can revive the dying Sensate order as the dominant order in the Western world. A partial patching up of its worst diseases and a slowing down of its disintegration is possible, but such operations cannot rejuvenate the moribund and "senile Sensate organism." First, I do not know a single case in the history of great societies and civilization wherein a moribund dominant order has been successfully rejuvenated. Such a miracle is as little possible as the rejuvenation of an old individual into a young man. Second, the very fact of the decay of any institution, value system, or order is a sure sign of the exhaustion of the fund of creative forces it had during the period of its domination. During its domination the Western Sensate order created magnificent achievements in science and technology, Sensate philosophy and fine arts, and Sensate politics and economics, but these achievements began to dry out in this century with the exception of science and technology. Even in these fields the recent achievements increasingly have tended to serve destructive rather than constructive purposes as exemplified by the use of nuclear, bacteriological, chemical, and other scientific discoveries for warfare and other destructive tasks. Any institution or order which is exhausted of its creative forces outlives its usefulness, becomes "dysfunctional," and in due time is removed from the stage of living historical reality-values into a museum of history.

My third and main reason for this prognosis is that the major postulate of the Sensate order (the sensory nature of true reality-value) has now been proven to be too narrow and quite inadequate. Its own emergence and growth at the end of the domination of the Ideational (religious) order of the Middle Ages was due to the analogous narrowness of the dominant Ideational order and the exhaustion of *its* creative potential. The Sensate order which emerged performed a vital correction of the inadequacies of the Ideational order and in its creative period released much new creative potential and gave to mankind magnificent achievements of Sensate human genius. Now, like the Ideational order in *its* uncreative phase, it is dying and bound to be replaced.

These considerations explain why I regard as improbable the revival and rejuvenation of a Sensate order as the dominant one in the remainder of this century and in the next one. In the more remote future, however, after the rise and decline of new Ideational, Integral, or Eclectic dominant orders, a new variation of Sensate order is very likely again to be dominant in the West. Indeed, its comparative growth in the East is quite probable and can be expected in a much shorter period of time.[9]

If the rejuvenation of the Sensate order as the way out of the present crisis of the Western world is not very probable, therefore, what are the chances of an *eclectic* pseudo-order becoming the next dominant order in the West? With our assumption of the continued creativity of the Western peoples the answer to this question is that the chances are very slim. An Eclectic culture and society represent a sort of a sociocultural "dump" filled with odds and ends of diverse, often contradictory, values, ideologies, behaviors, institutions, relationships, and movements. An eclectic order is a glorified disorder rather than a unified order of a great sociocultural system. Any great society and culture that ends its life by turning into a sort of long-term "dump" loses its individuality and becomes mere "civilizational fertilizer" and raw material for other civilizations and peoples. And any people or nation that cannot create a new sociocultural order in place of a disintegrated one ceases to be a leading "historical" society and becomes mere "ethnographic material" to be absorbed and used by other more creative peoples. With my assumption of the continued creativity of Western societies an end such as this is not probable.

This means that, given my assumptions, the new dominant order in the West must be either a new Ideational or a new Integral or some other basic unified order. My guess is that this new order is more likely to be a *new Integral order* than either an Ideational or any other type of great culture and society.[10]

In the form of "the second religiosity" (in Spengler's terms) a *temporary* revival of Ideational mentality and behavior is possible and even probable. But such a flare-up of Ideationality can hardly become a *long time* dominant order in the period under discussion. First, because the onesidedness and inadequacy of the medieval Ideational order are not forgotten by the present and the coming generations of the West. Second, because its defects and narrowness are demonstrated regularly in the contemporary world by the decline of the Oriental variation of Ideational order in such countries as Tibet, India, Ceylon, Burma, Taoist China, and other countries of the East. Until recently this order had been dominant in these countries. Despite its long domination it has not eliminated misery, poverty, ignorance, exploitation, the caste system, and a multitude of interpersonal and intergroup conflicts among the peoples of the Orient. Its long domination in these societies has not created either a heavenly or earthly paradise there. In recent decades this hitherto dominant order in the East has been rapidly disintegrating because of the exhaustion of its creative forces, just as the exhaustion of creative forces is causing the Sensate order in the West to crumble. In Japan and Communist China this order has already largely been replaced by a predominantly Sensate order, in capitalist-democratic form in Japan and in communist-totalitarian form in China. This spectacle of dying Ideational orders in the East can hardly inspire Western generations to revive this order as the dominant one in the decades to come.

Third, the most marvelous developments of today's and tomorrow's science and technology are a further gigantic obstacle to the re-enthronement of a new variation of this order in either the Occident or the Orient. By its very nature science refuses to acknowledge as true and valid any proposition that does not meet the scientific canon of rational and empirical verification. Many dogmas and beliefs, values and commandments, sacred rituals and mythologies of Ideational *Weltanschauung*, however, are given as absolute "revelations" of God (or God's equivalents) that can neither be doubted nor logically or empirically verified. Exactly because of this antagonism between scientifically verified truth and Ideational "revealed" dogma, a rapid development of scientific discoveries and inventions in the centuries from the thirteenth to the twentieth has been one of the decisive factors in the decline and demotion of many dogmas of Christianity in the West to the category of "blind beliefs," "errors," and "super-stitions." Through this demotion of Christian dogmas, rituals, precepts and values, the rapid growth of science played a most important role in the disintegration of the European Ideational order and in its subsequent replacement by a dominant Sensate order.[11]

Science, instead of being a handmaiden of religion and theology as it was in the early medieval centuries, has now become the epitome of verified knowledge and adequate truth. It is unlikely that during the next decades it will lose all of this great prestige. Therefore, as long as this gigantic epitome of verified knowledge (together with its practical application—technology) continues to develop, this development alone is sufficient to inhibit the elevation of a new Ideational order to a dominant position in the coming century.

The net result of the above considerations is that *the most probable dominant order of the next century is likely to be a new and great variation of the Integral (Idealistic) order* in the social, cultural, and personal life of the urbanized, industrialized, and technologically advanced societies of the West and also, but in a notably different form, in the societies of the East.

The Integral order is based upon the major principle that the *total* true reality-value is an "Infinite Manifold" of infinitely numerous and diverse qualitative and quantitative dimensions. In its total plenitude it hardly can be grasped adequately by to-day's finite human mind. However, being a conscious-creative part of it we can discern at least three main dimensions: (a) its sensory aspect, perceived by our sense organs and their extensions: microscopes, telescopes, radar, etc.; (b) its rational aspect, grasped by our rational, logico-mathematical thought; and (c) its most hidden, supersensory-superrational (but not supernatural) aspect, discovered by the genius's "intuition," "inspiration," and "enlightenment" (a channel of cognition and creativity quite different from sensory perception and logico-mathematical thought) in all creative fields of sociocultural cognition and creativity.[12]

Of many reasons for this prognosis I can mention here only one or two. Its premise is less narrow and more adequate than either the Ideational or Sensate premises. The Integral premise embraces the true parts of both of these premises and asserts the reality and value of sensory as well as of rational and super-sensory forms of being. Through its three channels of cognition and creativity [13]—the sensory, the rational, and the supersensory-superrational (mutually complementing and checking one another)—it enables us to cognize the manifold total reality more fully and to create reality-values more freely and fruitfully not only in the cognitive fields of science, technology, and philosophy but no less in the fields of aesthetic, moral, and religious values. In this way the Integral premise and order would reunite again the main reality-values of Truth, Goodness, and Beauty into one supreme unity or *summum bonum*.

This more adequate Integral premise allows us to build upon it a much richer, truer, more beautiful, and ethically nobler social, cultural, and personal way of life. Reunification of Truth, Goodness, and Beauty into one supreme *summum bonum* of reality-value tends to make any cognitive verity beautiful and good, any beauty true and good, and any moral goodness true and beautiful. Mutual complementation and control of these supreme reality-values would tend to prevent the production, diffusion, and fashionable acceptance of many pseudo-truths, ugly pseudo-beauties, and false moral and political precepts so luxuriously blossoming in our declining Sensate order today.

Such in brief are some of the basic characteristics of the Integral order. In the past these characteristics were displayed in Greek society and culture during the fifth century B.C. and in in an Integral order dominant in the thirteenth century in Europe. In a new creative variation these traits can be expected to be developed by the coming Integral order in the West as well as in the East.

With this basic and somewhat abstract background we can

now unfold in greater detail some of the more specific characteristics of the coming Integral order in its social, cultural, and personal life and organization.

### D. SOME ESSENTIAL CHARACTERISTICS OF INTEGRAL SOCIETY

1. Its total network of interpersonal and intergroup relationships consists mainly of what I call *familistic* relationships, exemplified by the relationship between members of a good family based on mutual, spontaneous love, sympathy, and aid; to a lesser extent of *contractual* relationships of the parties freely agreeing on an exchange of goods or services beneficial and profitable for each contracting party; and to a still smaller degree of *compulsory* relationships imposed coercively by one party upon another.[14] The proportion of familistic relationships in Integral society is much larger and that of coercive relationships much smaller than is the case in Sensate or Ideational societies. This means that neither a rampant selfish individualism nor a compulsory collective regimentation can proliferate in Integral society.

2. The prevalence of familistic relationships in the coming Integral society signifies that it will be not only a political but also an economic and sociocultural democracy or "big family," comparatively more free from exploitation, injustice, and striking inequalities than the Sensate, Ideational, or Eclectic societies.

(a) Economically it will be neither a capitalist nor a communist system but a system of Integral economy free from most of the defects of capitalist or communist (regimented) economies and incorporating most of the valuable features of both. It will endeavour to secure a decent standard of living for every one of its members. It will strive to combine the advantages of modern technological centralization, automation, large-scale production, and expert management with an autonomy of private groups and individuals in a number of industrial and economic enterprises; to merge the benefits of collectivism with those of freedom, dignity, initiative, and the self-realization of individuals; to reconcile an enlightened but somewhat rigid bureaucracy of expert managers with the creative initiative of persons and groups; to integrate social planning with spontaneity and constructive deviation; to harmonize radical equality with inequality of talent and merit; and to unify the responsibility of a society for each of its members with the individual's responsibility to himself and to his society.

Since the Integral order is likely to be largely free from destructive wars and bloody civil strife (intergroup conflicts being peacefully negotiated and resolved by the parties involved, by the government, by the United Nations, or by a Federal World Government), the coming Integral Society will not need to waste its scientific-technological inventiveness, its natural resources, its wealth, and its human members for devastating wars and conflicts. Its concentration on constructive economic activities beneficial to all its members can help to raise its population's standard of living to a notably higher level than has been possible for Sensate and Ideational societies of the past and in our time, with their economic activities and resources largely wasted in devastating wars and ferocious conflicts.

The higher economic level of Integral society will also be achieved on the part of its creative inventors, scientists, organizers, managers, and the rank and file of membership, by the inspiration, ethos, and pathos involved in serving the well-being of the *whole* society. We must not undervalue (as we often do) this kind of incentive and motivation for the improvement of economic life.

(b) Its political organization on a national and international scale is likely to be marked by the following innovations. First, by the establishment of a World Federal Government for the management of a limited number of international and intergroup relationships and objectives in which the well-being of all mankind is involved, and particularly for the prevention of intergroup conflicts or their peaceable resolution. Second, the political regime of the coming Integral society is likely to be democratic, but notably different from existing "democratic" regimes. The latter have degenerated tangibly from "government of the people, by the people, and for the people," into "government of politicians, by politicians, and for politicians." Most existing so-called democratic governments, which allegedly are elected by "universal suffrage," in reality are nominated and picked by a small oligarchic group of the power elite. The democratic privilege of voting by all citizens is reduced practically to putting their mark on the ballot for nominees whom they neither have nominated nor really know in view of the fictitious knowledge of the candidates' "image" which the gigantic, brainwashing propaganda machinery of the power elite impresses upon them. Nor do the nominees, when elected, feel at all obliged to keep the "high-falutin" promises made during the election campaign. Finally, most of the elected members of the government really know very little about the complex matters on which they have to make decisions; most contemporary politicians are in fact "inflated ignoramuses" in this regard.

These and other reasons explain why there has been a degeneration of truly democratic government into a government of politicians who often lack the competence, wisdom, and moral integrity necessary for a socially useful discharge of their duties.

The existing democratic-autocratic mechanisms for electing members of the ruling group have become dysfunctional and have ceased to select the best persons for government leadership. It is no wonder, therefore, that the recent and existing democratic governments have failed to perform their creative functions no less than the autocratic ruling groups usually associated with communism and fascism. They did not prevent two devastating world wars, a legion of smaller wars and "police actions," an endless parade of revolutions and revolts, an increase of crime, neurosis and psychosis, and so on.

Despite the apocalyptic price paid by mankind for these and many other failures of the "modern governments," mankind still has neither lasting peace, nor security, nor freedom from misery, nor decent conditions for its vital, moral, cultural, and economic well-being and creativity. If anything, recent and existing—democratic and autocratic—governments have brought the human race to the brink of a suicidal catastrophe which might incinerate this beautiful planet and terminate man's creative history altogether.

There is no need to argue further the point of why such incompetent, inept, and factually undemocratic governments cannot be accepted and established in the coming Integral society. The most serious and complex problems of the new order can be solved successfully only by a "government of Scientists, Saints (moral leaders), and Sages" (abbreviated as "Government of SSS"). Such a government will consist of the best scientific experts, of moral leaders (of the type of M. Gandhi or A. Schweitzer or Pope John XXIII) who can guide and prevent a misuse of science by experts, and of creative sages (wise philosophers, leaders of spirituality, fine arts and literature and inventive geniuses) who can help in the apprehension and comprehension of the total situation of human affairs in the world or in a given society and can suggest new ideas for the solution of the great problems of Integral society. This form of government would be not only more competent, creative, and better prepared to solve fruitfully complex problems but also, if its members were to be elected by distinguished bodies of scientists and of moral leaders and by the most distinguished religious, philosophical, artistic, and literary organizations, it could be a much more democratic government elected by a larger group of the creative elector-leaders than the contemporary "governments of politicians, by politicians, and for politicians." The latter governments, as was pointed out above, are nominated and "elected" *de facto* by a much smaller group of the elite, most of whom are merely influential politicians.

In addition, universal suffrage could function in this sort of political regime more adequately than in the regimes of our time. Universal suffrage could be demonstrated regularly and frequently in the form of referendum polls of all citizens, who would express their approval or disapproval of important measures or policies of their governent of SSS. A negative vote on the part of a considerable majority of the voters could act as a touchstone and be given the power of veto. This aspect of universal suffrage makes such a government still more democratic than any "democratic" government of politicians of our time.

The outlined government of SSS may appear fantastic and unreal to many. Yet in its first aspect, as a "government of scientists," it already exists and plays an important and ever larger role in all present governments. Today's politicians and rulers have largely become mere figurehead-executors of the "silent orders" of science and technology. Recent scientific discoveries and inventions have made obsolete most of what the top-ruling politicians and military leaders learned two or three decades ago. For example, none of the top politicians and military professionals before 1935–1940 had the slightest idea about nuclear weapons, missiles, and other modern means of warfare, nor had their professional training prepared them for leadership in this regard. The invention of nuclear weapons and other nuclear, bacteriological, chemical, and physical means of warfare made obsolete most of their military training and its strategies and tactics. Before 1940 none of the leaders, such as Truman, Churchill, Stalin, Hitler, Eisenhower, or any of the other generals, admirals, marshals, and top politicians had even the fuzziest notion of atomic, hydrogenic, and outer-space policies and strategies. Each of the recent important scientific discoveries has forced them to replace their outdated policies and plans with new and quite different diplomatic, military, economic, educational, public-health, agricultural, and other policies.

There is hardly any doubt that the role of science and scientists in governments will be growing rapidly, while the role of incompetent politicians will be progressively decreasing. Even the politician's present role of being a figurehead executing the silent orders of science is likely to die out; incompetent politicians have become useless in this role, which can be discharged better by scientists themselves.

With some modification these conclusions can be applied also to moral leaders and sages as active participants in Integral government. Their membership in it is advisable to complement the special knowledge of scientists and to prevent the misuse of that knowledge for evil or destructive purposes. The knowledge of scientific experts is often too narrow and limited to knowledge of a special problem. Such specialized knowledge needs to be supplemented by the sage's wider vision of the vaster reality-values of which a given special problem is but a part. This vaster understanding of sages fruitfully complements and corrects the too narrow knowledge of scientist-experts.

In their empirical form science and technology are morally and socially neutral. Almost any scientific discovery or invention can be and has been used for good and evil purposes. The prevention of the misuse of scientific discoveries by "morally neutral" scientists (and the prevention of the common transformation of scientist-rulers into oligarchic technocrats) makes necessary the membership of moral leaders and sages in Integral government.

These brief comments elucidate somewhat my guess about the kind of government that will predominate in Integral society.[15]

E. SOME ESSENTIAL TRAITS OF INTEGRAL CULTURE

Because the basic postulate of the Integral order asserts the reality of *sensory* dimensions and values, science and technology will continue their creative growth. However, since they are mainly focused on cognition and invention in just this one area of reality-value, there are bound to be two important differences in their functioning in Integral society. Integral science and technology will largely shun discoveries and inventions which have destructive purposes of "overkill" and the endangering of human well-being. In the Integral theory of true reality-value the sensory dimension is only one of three main dimensions and values; and since sensory cognition is only one of three main channels of cognition and creativity, scientific-sensory cognition and creativity will be working hand in hand with logico-mathe-matical and intuitional ways of cognition and creativity. Each of these channels will be checking and complementing the cognitive and creative results of the other two channels, and only the hypotheses or propositions approved by all three channels will be regarded as fully validated and true.

This means that in the Integral order there would be no grounds for antagonism between Science and Philosophy, Science and Religion, Science and Fine Arts and so on, insofar as Science concentrates mainly on cognition of the empirical (sensory) aspect, Philosophy on the rational dimension, Religion on the supersensory-superrational, and Fine Arts on cognition and creativity of the concrete forms of the total, unified reality-value. In this way the three main reality-values of the total reality and *summum bonum*—Truth, Goodness, and Beauty—will be reunited again into One Supreme Reality-Value: each constructive scientific achievement also will be contributing to philosophico-religious and aesthetic cognition-creativity of the inexhaustible total reality-value, and vice versa. In all these fields, as a result of this unification and cooperation of scientific, philosophico-religious, aesthetic and ethical cognition and creativity, a notable upsurge can be expected of cognitive and creative achievements at their noblest and best, paralleled by a decline of pseudo-scientific, pseudo-philosophical and pseudo-religious, pseudo-aesthetic-ethical-political and economic trash which is flooding the declining Sensate order of our age. In Saint-Simon's terms, the coming of Integral order will usher the human universe into a new "Organic" period instead of the "Critical" one in which we live.

With proper modification the same can be said of the currents of philosophical, religious, ethical, artistic, literary, political, economic, and social thought of the Integral order. They all are bound to have a brilliant renaissance; the whole social, cultural, and personal life will be elevated to a much nobler, freer, and resplendent level; man himself also will be uplifted to his highest creative self. Enjoying fully the true values of sensory, rational, and supersensory-superrational orders, man probably will be able to transcend and control his beastly impulses, animal propensities, and acquired antisocial and selfish tendencies much more successfully than he can now. In his mentality, behavior, and relationship to his fellow men and the world at large he will regard every human being as an end-value that should not be used as a mere means for anything or anybody. He is likely to be a real *homo sapiens*, morally and socially responsible to himself, to his fellow men, to the world at large, and to God as a creative *summum bonum*. Finally, Integral man probably can achieve much deeper peace and more sublime happiness than contemporary man.

Under the assumptions made at the beginning of this paper, such appears to me to be the shape and make-up of the coming Integral order. If these assumptions are uncertain or wrong (as some of them may be, like the nonexplosion of world wars or a continued high-grade creativity of the Western population), then most of the prognoses are bound to be uncertain and wrong. I hope, however, that in these optimistic assumptions and prognoses I may be as lucky as I was in the pessimistic prognoses which I made in the nineteen twenties and thirties—and that my prognosis of the Integral order to come will be confirmed by the objective course of human history for the end of this century and for the twenty-first.

Let me end this prognosis with an additional and final one: Assuming that my guesses turn out to be correct, after the coming Integral order realizes all its creative potential it also will decline in due time and be replaced by a different dominant order!

NOTES

1. See on this P. Sorokin, "Creativity in Human History," *Sociologia Internationalis*, Band I (1963), pp. 55–56; also P. Sorokin, *Sociological Theories of Today* (New York: Harper & Row, 1966), pp. 611–613; K. Popper, *The Poverty of Historicism* (Boston: Beacon Press, 1957), Chapter 1, et passim.

2. Almost all of these "guesses" have come to pass. See these forecastings in P. Sorokin, *Social and Cultural Dynamics* (New York: American Book Co., 1937–1941 and the Bedminster Press, 1962), Vol. III, Chapter 16 and Vol. IV, Chapter 17; and *Crisis of Our Age* (New York: E. P. Dutton, 1941 and 1957).

3. See on these trends P. Sorokin, *The Basic Trends of Our Time* (New Haven: College and University Press, 1964), Chapter 1.

4. See on these modifications, *Ibid.*, Chapter 2.

5. See this diagnosis in my *Social and Cultural Dynamics*, in all four volumes; *Crisis of Our Age, Society, Culture and Personality* (New York: Harper & Row, 1947); "The Western Religion and Morality of Today," *Internationales Jahrbuch für Religionssoziologie*, Band II (1966), Westdeutscher Verlag, Koln und Opladen; *Sociological Theories of Today* (New York: Harper & Row, 1966).

6. See on this my *Dynamics*, Vol. III, Chapters 9–14.

7. See on this struggle *The Basic Trends of Our Time*, pp. 25–60.

8. Though today's prevalent opinion is that the tempi of all sociocultural changes in modern times are greatly accelerated, this opinion remains but an unproved belief. A study of this problem by A. Kroeber and other investigators, including myself, has led to the conclusion that the tempi of basic changes in sociocultural orders have been about the same in the past as in recent times. "The data indicate rather conclusively that the rate [of change] has not gained speed. So far as high quality growths [of sociocultural systems and values] are concerned, they seem to take about as long now as they did one or two thousand years ago." A. Kroeber, *Configurations of Culture Growth* (Berkeley and Los Angeles: University of California Press, 1944), pp. 804, 808–810; for my similar conclusions see my *Dynamics*, Vol. IV, Chapter 11.

9. "To build up the new integral order the Eastern peoples in the near future will be focusing their efforts on the improvement of their material conditions along the ennoblement and integral reconstruction of their rational and ideational values." To build an integral order the Western peoples will increasingly "spiritualize" and "idealize" the Western world. *The Basic Trends of Our Time*, p. 71; see there Chapter 2 on this problem.

10. Though in my *Dynamics* I have shown that in the history of the Greco-Roman and Western culture the succession of the main orders has always been the same, namely: Sensate-Ideational-Idealistic, or, what is the same, Ideational-Idealistic (Integral)-Sensate, in analyzing this problem I stressed that this order is in no way universal for all societies and cultures. See the *Dynamics*, Vol. IV, pp. 770–773.

11. See a detailed analysis and historical-statistical evidence for these statements in my *Dynamics*, Vol. II, Chapters 1–3; and my article "The Western Religion and Morality of Today" in the *International Yearbook for the Sociology of Religion*, Westdeutsche Verlag, Koln und Opladen, Band II (1966), pp. 9–50.

12. See a development of this premise and of integral cognition, creativity, and sociocultural order in my *Dynamics*, Vol. IV, Chapter 16; *The Ways and Power of Love* (Chicago: Henry Regnery Co., 1967), Chapters 5, 6, and 7; *The Basic Trends of Our Time*, Chapters 1 and 2; *Sociological Theories of Today*, pp. 630–634 et passim; P. Allen (editor), *Pitirim A. Sorokin in Review* (Durham: Duke University Press, 1963), pp. 372–400.

13. Cognition and creativity are twins: any creativity is a discovery of the hidden, potential form of a reality-value, and any scientific or other discovery is also a bringing into the light a feature of a hitherto unknown and hidden reality-value. Any creativity is a discovery and any discovery is a creativity.

14. See a detailed analysis of familistic, contractual, and compulsory relationships and a fluctuation of their relative importance in the total network of social relationships of the Greco-Roman and the Western societies during the past twenty-five centuries in my *Dynamics*, Vol. III, Chapters 1–4; *Crisis of Our Age*, Chapters 5 and 6.

15. For further elaboration of the economic and political regimes to come see my *Power and Morality* (Boston: Porter Sargent Co., 1959), Chapters X, XI, XII; also my *Reconstruction of Humanity* (Boston: Beacon Press, 1948), Chapters 9, 10, 11.

## ABOUT THE CONTRIBUTORS

Kenneth E. Boulding is Professor of Economics at the University of Colorado.

Lewis A. Coser is Distinguished Service Professor of Sociology at the State University of New York, Stony Brook.

Lyle C. Fitch is President of the Institute of Public Administration, New York City.

August Heckscher is Administrator of Recreation and Cultural Affairs and Commissioner of Parks, New York City. He was formerly Director of the Twentieth Century Fund.

Alfred J. Kahn is Professor of Social Work at Columbia University.

Norton E. Long is Professor of Government at the University of Illinois.

Ian McHarg is Chairman of the Department of Landscape Architecture and Regional Planning at the University of Pennsylvania.

Arthur T. Naftalin is Mayor of the City of Minneapolis.

David Popenoe is Director of Academic Affairs at the Urban Studies Center and a member of the faculty of Livingston College, Rutgers University.

The late Pitirim A. Sorokin was Emeritus Professor of Sociology at Harvard University.

Harold Taylor, educator and author, was formerly President of Sarah Lawrence College.